The
BLINDFOLDED
MARRIAGE

The BLINDFOLDED MARRIAGE

EVER FEEL LIKE YOUR RELATIONSHIP IS HARDER THAN IT SHOULD BE?

JONATHAN HOOVER

Associate Pastor and Couples Pastor of NewSpring Church
Wichita, KS

Published by J & W Publishers, Derby, KS

All anecdotes related to Jonathan's coaching ministry represent a mosaic of multiple couples' experiences. In these stories, identities are fictional and details have been changed in order to ensure anonymity.

ISBN: 978-0-9860576-3-2
Library of Congress Control Number: 2013917936

Cover Design: TJ Nix
Publisher: J&W Publishing
Editor: Tiffany Nix
1. Marriage 2. Relationships 3. Christianity.
First Edition

To Wendy, the beautiful woman I've been privileged to call my wife and share my life with for the past ten years. Thank you for being my encourager, confidant, and best friend. You inspired me to write this book, and I hope I can find a way to live up to what I have written.

CONTENTS

FORWARD

When I was asked if I could write the Introduction for Jonathan Hoover's book, *The Blindfolded Marriage*, I began to think that this is a subject that I can always use improvement in. Little did I know that as I began to turn the pages that God would use the book you are holding in your hand to speak so deeply in my heart. As Jonathan began to give examples of couples he has counseled, I could see Janet and me in almost all of them. And I might add it was extremely helpful to see how I often times respond without really listening.

We have all heard that communication is one of the most helpful and needed components in marriage, however to be instructed as to what all that entails unfolds in the pages of this book. Jonathan does a masterful job of connecting the dots as to what it means to be one, what it means to really listen and how to listen to hear what is really being said in order that we may have course correction to lead to a healthy relationship. I would purchase this book if it were only for the examples and illustrations.

I must confess after reading the book I had a talk with my wife and shared with her the valuable principles I had learned. I even asked her to forgive me for the ways I had responded to her conversations with me because of my lack of understanding. This book will give you clarity in marriage that will be an impetus and help drive the desire to be healthier as husband and wife.

I do not like to read because I love reading; I read because of the discipline to be more of a godly man which certainly speaks deeply into being a godly husband. I have often said that if you can be a good Christian at home, you can be a good Christian anywhere. However, if you are not a good Christian at home you may not be a good Christian anywhere. This book starts in the first institution that God ever created. It helps you to have a more solid foundation upon which to build. I have loved my wife for 43 years but this book has helped to understand how I can love, support, encourage and comfort her in even greater ways.

My heartfelt gratitude to the author of *The Blindfolded Marriage*, Jonathan Hoover, for thinking through, for illustrating, for lifting out Biblical text that gives stories of men and women and how their approach caused most of their problems. His approach provides resolution, to these problems, in order for us to lead a healthier life. This in turn gives the potential for healthier couples in order to be a witness and example for the generations that follow.

Read this book, I promise you will recommend it to your friends.

Johnny M. Hunt
Former President, Southern Baptist Convention
Pastor, First Baptist Church Woodstock, Woodstock, GA

Chapter 1

BLINDFOLDS

Do you ever feel like your marriage is a little more difficult than it should be? Do you ever feel like it shouldn't be so hard for you and your spouse to communicate, compromise, or resolve conflict? If so, the truth is that you're probably right. It's very likely that your marriage could be easier than it is now. Marriage (like any close relationship) will always bring difficulties and struggles. But, wouldn't you like to keep those to a minimum? That's what this book is all about. I'm going to share the secret to reducing the difficulty in your marriage, and along the way, we'll talk about how you can achieve your full potential by getting on board with God's plan for your relationship.

Let's talk for a minute about blindfolds. I'm convinced blindfolds were invented because adults were bored at their kids' birthday parties and needed something to laugh at. The solution: cover up a little kid's eyes, spin them around a few times, and give them a stick to try to smash a piñata. The result? Instant entertainment. Blindfolds have one purpose—*to make an easy task nearly impossible*

by taking away a person's ability to see what's in front of them.
Smashing a piñata or pinning the tail on a paper donkey
is an easy task if you can see. Blindfolded, though, the
level of difficulty skyrockets.

At kids' birthday parties, blindfolds add to the fun. In
adult relationships, they can be downright infuriating.
And Satan uses "blindfolds" every day to ruin marriages.
He finds ways to keep husbands and wives from truly
"seeing" each other, and every time he succeeds, a marriage
becomes much more difficult. The good news is that you
don't have to spend your marriage in the dark. You have
the power to choose to see reality in your relationship. If
you do, simple tasks become easy again.

So if you've been discouraged about your marriage, this
might be a moment for you to take a deep breath and
realize *things can be okay.* If you've had moments where
you've felt overwhelmed, underpowered and out of solutions, it's time for you to realize that you *can* be the spouse
you hope to be. Tell that overwhelmed part of yourself
that you're not struggling because of what you *can't do*,
but because of what you *don't see.*

IT'S NOT WHAT YOU CAN'T DO, BUT RATHER WHAT YOU DON'T SEE

Imagine that we were able to find the most talented quarterback in the National Football League. This guy knows
how to dominate the game, and is basically unstoppable.
Now, imagine that as we send this player out on the field

to play against a rival team, we force him to wear a blind-fold. No matter how exceptional his skills are, he will fail. He will not look like a professional football player. In fact, he'll probably look like a complete idiot. He'll have no idea where to throw the ball because he can't see his receivers. He won't know where to run because he can't see the end zone or the sidelines. He can't stand still, because there are linebackers on the opposing team who would like to crush him into tiny quarterback pieces. I predict that our blindfolded star quarterback will let the team down—big time.

Now, imagine that blindfolded football player came to you and said, "I'm a terrible football player. I just can't play the game well. I can't throw, I can't run, I think I should just give it up. Maybe I'm incompatible with the game of football." Of course you would be quick to argue with him, "It's not that you can't play... it's that you can't see! It's not about what you're not able to do. It's about the fact that your vision is obstructed. Once you can see clearly again, you'll be able to play well again."

See where I'm going with this? Give yourself the same pep-talk about your marriage. At times, you may feel like there are many things you can't do well in your relation-ship. Sometimes those thoughts can make you feel like a complete failure. But you're not a failure. Even if you and your spouse experience struggles, God has given you the abilities to make your marriage incredible. You just need to see clearly. Perhaps, like our football player, you've spent part of your marriage blindfolded. It's possible that during your marriage you've struggled to really understand where your spouse is coming from. Maybe they've struggled to "see" you, too. The Bible says that when our vision is obstructed things can get chaotic.

> *Proverbs 29:18 (NIV)*
> *18 Where there is no revelation, people cast off restraint; but blessed is the one who heeds wisdom's instruction.*

A basic paraphrase of this verse is: "When you don't really know what you're dealing with, you can expect chaotic results. If you're willing to understand the truth and act accordingly, your future will be bright."

Just like the football player that faces chaos because he can't see the action on the field, many of us face chaotic moments in our relationships because we fail to see and understand the underlying problems that keep us from being the spouse God wants us to be. When we lose our *vision* in life—when we don't clearly see reality—we stop acting like we know what we're doing. Even though we're good at communicating, our desperation takes us out of our zone of effectiveness and we start saying and doing things that are counterproductive. Even though we're good at compromising, the desperation tells us to hold to our rights to the bitter end. Even though we're good at forgiving, the blindfold leaves us vulnerable and desperate, and we feel that forgiveness isn't an option.

You're probably much better at this "marriage thing" than you think. Is it possible you're "playing blindfolded?" Is it possible that you get desperate sometimes and that takes you out of your effective zone? Could the same thing be happening to your spouse? It's time to take the blindfold off. It's time to see your marriage for what it is. It's time for you to get to know your spouse all over again.

GETTING RID OF OLD UNDERSTANDINGS...

If you've been in your relationship for a while, it could be that you've already tried to figure out what you're dealing with when you hit a rough patch. Maybe when you and your spouse struggle, it leads you to think that your personalities are mismatched. Maybe you've concluded that you're incompatible with each other. Or maybe you've decided that your spouse's parents spoiled them or set them up for failure in some significant way. Maybe you've decided that your difficulties stem from a lack of communication. Or maybe you've started *labeling* your spouse. Maybe you've decided they're hurtful, unyielding, selfish or narcissistic.

My question is this: What are you going to *do* with those conclusions? Say your personalities aren't a perfect fit. What then? You can't change either of your personalities. Say your spouse's parents really did a number on them. What then? You can't go back in time and change their upbringing. And what will you do with all those labels? If your spouse is narcissistic, harsh, or unyielding, you can't *make them* be different.

Labeling your spouse won't help you do the right thing. Neither will pointing fingers and placing blame. In this book, we're only looking for understandings that will help you tap into your *own* God-given ability to succeed. Just as I believe that with the right field of vision our skilled football player will succeed, I believe that if you have the field of vision you need, you will also succeed.

THREE STORIES...

The following stories help illustrate my point. As you read these three vignettes, you'll notice that the "big issues" these couples face can be distilled down to one main problem: a lack of understanding. In each case, it was a failure to "see" the other person that caused the fireworks. Sure, there's a "what" in every fight—what was done or said that caused the conflict. But notice that in each of these stories the "why" is much more important.

David and Penny

David and Penny had been married for about a year when they hit a major marital snag. In the middle of the night Penny woke up with a fever. After about half an hour of chills and nausea, she decided to wake up her husband who had been sleeping deeply.

"I'm sorry you're feeling bad, sweetheart," he said, "Is there anything I can do?"

She shook her head, "No, I don't think so. I just need you to be here with me."

"No problem, sweetheart. I'm here for you." Then he rolled over and went back to sleep.

The next day, David went to work. Penny stayed home and made an afternoon trip to the doctor. Later, when David arrived home, Penny was back in bed. He poked his head around the bedroom door and said, "Hey, babe, do you need anything?"

She shook her head again and said, "No; I guess not."

David spent the rest of the night in the living room watching TV. Just before David would have gone to sleep, he heard his wife sobbing in the bedroom. He asked her what she was upset about.

The conversation went like this:

David: What's the matter?

Penny: Nothing.

David: I'm not buying that… are you okay?

Penny: I'd be better if you acted like you care about me.

David: What? I don't care about you? I picked up your prescription, didn't I? I offered to take you to the doctor, didn't I? I keep asking if there's anything I can do... what do you want from me?

Penny: I want you to treat me like I'm important to you.

David: I do treat you that way. It's just not good enough for you.

Penny: Oh, sure. Now it's my fault. I just wanted you to be there for me.

David: I have been here for you. I came straight home from work and I've offered to get you anything you need. I can't believe you're mad at me. I've done nothing wrong. You are the most unreasonable woman I have ever met. Have a nice night.

So David leaves feeling like he can never be good enough for Penny, and Penny feels like David doesn't value her or see her as important.

What David doesn't get about Penny

Penny lost her mom at an early age. She was very close to her father. Whenever Penny would get sick as a child, her father would go to the little Chinese restaurant on the corner to get her what they both referred to as "the best chicken noodle soup in the universe." When Penny grew up and went away to college, she missed her dad, but whenever she would get sick he would overnight a bowl of the chicken noodle soup to her dorm room.

Now her dad had also passed away, but she still felt his love for her. In her mind, true love looks like "the best chicken noodle soup in the universe" when you're sick. She knew her husband didn't know about the soup, and she didn't expect him to read her mind. She just hoped that David would find his own special way of making her feel better. It didn't happen, and she felt sad and alone.

What Penny doesn't get about David

David is completely intimidated by this scenario. David barely knows which medicine to take when he gets a headache. He's definitely never had to "take care of" someone when they're sick. This is at least a mile or two outside his comfort zone. But he's pretty sure he's doing okay. When he sees Penny so upset, and she says it's his fault, he feels like a complete failure.

What do you think? If Penny and David are truly nice people who love each other and want their marriage to succeed, does Penny want David to feel like a failure? Does David want Penny to feel alone and sad?

Joel and Susan

Joel and Susan have been married for fifteen years and they always fight the same way. The topic of the fight changes, but the pattern stays the same. Susan gets upset about something and wants to talk about it — right now. Joel will usually hang in there for a minute or two, but once he realizes that Susan is mad, he bails. A good example of this would be the time Joel bought a 60" TV without talking to Susan about it first.

Susan: I can't believe you, Joel! How could you spend this kind of money and not even bother to pick up the phone and talk to me about it first?

Joel: I did pick up the phone and call. You didn't answer—as usual.

Susan: What, and it would have killed you to wait a couple hours to purchase your precious TV set? C'mon.

Joel tries to walk out of the room.

Susan: Where are you going?

Joel: Anywhere but here. Just leave me alone.

Joel keeps trying to walk away. Susan is following close behind.

Susan: Oh, yeah. There he goes again, the *disappearing husband*. Why can't you stay and talk to me about this?

Joel walks out the front door and heads for his car. He yells back over his shoulder.

Joel: Cause you're flipping out again. Leave me alone!

Susan yells back (loud enough for the neighbors to hear).

Susan: I'm flipping out because you were a jerk! I have a right to flip out. Don't expect your TV to be here when you get back!

Joel rolls down his window as he drives away and yells.

Joel: LEAVE ME ALONE!

When Joel comes home, they don't talk for the rest of the evening. Eventually they'll get tired of the mutual silence and they'll forget about the argument. There is no resolution to their problem. They spend their life hitting the "snooze" button on their conflict. It's as if when they get into a fight, an "alarm bell" sounds that shatters the calm they both enjoy. When they realize they can't figure out how to turn off the alarm, they hit the snooze. The alarm will sound again, but they wait until later to deal with it. They'll have this same fight—or one just like it—over and over again. Nothing seems to change.

What Susan doesn't get about Joel

When Joel sees Susan get mad at him, something deep inside of him panics. He desperately wants to know that Susan approves of him. When he sees the intensity of her upset feelings towards him, he feels that she doesn't like him. He's sure that she thinks he's an idiot. He feels like there's no good way to respond. What is he supposed to say? Is he supposed to admit to being an idiot? If he did, would that make her less mad? Probably not. He feels like the best thing he can do is hunker down and find a safe corner of the world to "hide out" until she's less mad.

What Joel doesn't get about Susan

Susan has *no interest* in getting Joel to see himself as a failure. She doesn't see him that way. She just wants to be *heard*. When Joel tries to end a discussion by saying, "I'm not talking about this anymore," or when he tries to leave the room, something deep inside Susan panics. Susan didn't bring up the issue of the TV because she wanted to make her husband feel bad. She brought it up because the situation was making *her* feel bad. In this case, the TV purchase scared her a little bit. When Joel made a large purchase and Susan wasn't even consulted, it made her feel completely out of the "big decisions" loop. That's scary to her.

When Susan tries to talk to Joel about the TV and he keeps walking away, it confirms Susan's worst fear. *He doesn't care about how I feel,* she thinks. *Not only will he make decisions without letting me be involved, he won't let me talk to him about how much that hurts me.* Then, for her, it triggers some of the scariest thoughts a wife can have. *He'll never understand me. He'll never hear me. The only one who will care about me is me.*

What do you think? Do you think that Susan really wants Joel to feel like an idiot? Do you think Joel wants Susan to feel alone and unheard?

Jonathan and Wendy
(This one's about my wife and I)

This past summer I started running. Since I'm off-the-charts ADD, I love having that time with just me and the pavement. It's time when I can focus with no distractions. I found out early on that there was a mobile app for running. I could track my routes, check my speed, and determine my distance. I love this app. I decided that there was no point in running unless you push yourself to the max. Being the typical guy, I needed someone to compete with. Since I was running alone, my only option was to compete with myself. Each night, I tried hard to beat the previous night's "records." I checked the app to make sure I was pushing myself to run faster and farther than ever before.

Meanwhile, my wife noticed that each night when I came in from running, I looked worse than the previous night. When I first started running, I would come in and talk about how great I felt. "That was a fantastic run. I'm feeling really good…" As I kept pushing myself in the days and weeks ahead, things changed. I got to the point where, at the end of my run, I would kind of stumble in the door, lay face down on the carpet, and thank God the run was over. This was all relatively disconcerting to my wife.

One night, I did it. I ran farther than ever before. I ran faster than ever before. I had run for a little over an hour and covered 6.8 miles.

As I came in the door, I said to my wife, "Can you believe it? I covered 6.8 miles! How about that?"

To which my wife had this response: "I'm not impressed by that."

I was blown away. *How could she say that?*

She continued, "You're going to kill yourself out there… 6.8 miles is crazy for you. What can I say? I'm not impressed."

I was livid.

I stomped down the stairs to take a shower. I couldn't imagine how my wife could say such a thing. How disrespectful! Doesn't she know that guys have an inner drive to achieve and take on ridiculous challenges? Doesn't she know that I'm a competitive guy? What's wrong with that? This is her fault. I can't win with her. She doesn't want me to be lazy, but if I exercise and push myself to the limit she's not happy then. She can't be pleased. (At least that's how it felt).

And then it started to make sense…

I asked myself, what am I going to do with that? Say she *was* disrespectful. What then? How does my assuming that help the situation? Say she *doesn't* understand my competitive nature. What then? Do I have some magic wand I can wave to make her feel differently? No. Then what do I have?

I have one basic realization. I must be missing something. If my wife is a good woman (and she is), and if she loves me (and she does), then there must be something I don't understand about the conversation we just had. I started to ask myself, *What did I miss? What don't I understand? Did my wife give me any hint about the reason she didn't think much of my run that evening?*

How about when she said, "You're going to kill yourself out there… 6.8 miles is crazy for you." That's it! I got out of the shower, ran up the stairs and asked Wendy, "Were you scared something bad was going to happen to me? That I would get hurt? Was that why you said you weren't impressed by my run?" She responded with an immediate, "Yes. I don't want anything bad to happen to you. I don't want to lose you."

Wow. I thought my wife was being hurtful to me, when she was actually paying me a huge compliment. Her saying, "I'm not impressed by your run," was the same thing as saying, "I'm not going to be to thrilled about anything that could take you away from me. I love you too much for that." It sounded disrespectful at first, but it was actually a very sweet thing for my wife to say.

If Penny and David really understood each other, they could have avoided the pain of the "chicken soup debacle of 2009." If Joel and Susan really "got" each other—if they really knew what it was like to be the other person—they would not be stuck in this dead-end pattern of conflict. When Wendy said, "I'm not impressed by your run," I would not have reacted badly, because I would have understood where she was coming from.

NAVIGATING THE MINEFIELD

Maybe you're not a sports fan, and the blindfolded quarterback image doesn't work for you. Think of it this way. Doing everyday life with your spouse can sometimes be kind of like walking through a minefield, right? You have to be very careful where you step. Sometimes you get "blown up" for no reason. You know the mines are there, but you don't know where they are. They surprise you, and it's hard to know how to respond. This is why people sometimes talk about "walking on eggshells" with each other. They're very aware that one "false step" can be devastating.

Luke and Deborah know all about this "navigating the minefield" business. They were truly a fun couple to work with. They had been going through some minor struggles, and I was doing my best to give them good coaching. One day when they came in, however, I could tell something was really wrong. I asked if they would share it with me. Deborah told me they recently attended the Christmas party for Luke's work. The evening had gone quite well, but at the end, she noticed one of Luke's female co-workers was giving him "the look." Luke didn't see "the look," but Deborah spotted it immediately.

When Luke and Deborah got in the car, Deborah told Luke that this other gal was bad news and that he should stay away from her.

Luke was totally taken by surprise. He immediately pushed back. He thought, *how dare she tell me who I can or can't be around? I'm a faithful husband. I've always been totally devoted to Deborah.* Luke couldn't believe what he was hearing. He responded by telling Deborah that she was overreacting, and then listed the good qualities of the woman in question. When Deborah saw this other woman looking at her husband, she was upset. Now that it sounds like Luke is defending her, *and* telling her how "great" she is, Deborah is hitting a level of desperate that only another woman who has walked a mile in her shoes would understand.

Luke and Deborah are both doing a little time in the minefield. Luke can't believe Deborah is upset over "nothing." Deborah, on the other hand, can't understand why Luke doesn't believe her and won't consider her feelings. Additionally, she's noticed that he is now mad at *her*—another thing she doesn't understand.

Luke and Deborah are doing marriage blindfolded. They have lost track of what it's like to be the other person, and they are clinging to their own view of the situation.

You can't play football blindfolded, you can't walk through a minefield without getting blown up, and you can't do marriage without learning to understand your spouse at a very basic level. You need to be able to understand their fears, their hurts, and their needs. If you are able to really "get" them, you will be able to be the kind of spouse God has called you to be.

A WORKING KNOWLEDGE

If this were a book about understanding how to work on automobiles, I would not be able to give you instructions for every make and model of vehicle. Such a task would be nearly impossible. What I would do, if this were a book about cars, would be to describe the basics of what makes a car run. I would share with you the technology that most cars have in common, and give you the chance to take that knowledge and apply it to the specific make and model you're working on. For instance, I might not be able to give you a full description of the way your specific engine works, but I could tell you that your engine won't run without the correct mixture of air, fuel, and spark.

In many ways, this book takes a similar approach in discussing the basics of how to understand your spouse. There is no way I could write a book that would be the definitive guide to your specific spouse. But what I can do is give you some basic concepts that will be true no matter who you married. Just as an internal combustion engine needs air, fuel, and spark to function properly, your spouse has basic needs that must be met. In each of the following chapters, we will discuss those needs and talk about how you can *understand* them.

I know that you've met your spouse. My goal in the next seven chapters is to *introduce* them to you. I hope that after you've read this book, you'll understand your spouse in ways you do not now. Even though the concepts we'll cover seem basic, they are as pivotal as the elements of combustion. Without them, your marriage will not work. Look at each chapter as a journey of discovery. As we cover concepts like trust, teamwork, comfort, support, acceptance, respect, and desire, be open to learning new things about your spouse, and perhaps even yourself.

Phil. 1:9 (NLT)
I pray that your love will overflow more and more, and that you will **keep on growing in knowledge and understanding**.
[Emphasis added]

Dear God,
As I start out on this journey to understand my spouse, I pray You will give me grace to "see." I know that You can help me understand my spouse, and as I read the pages of this book, I pray You'll help me identify and understand the truths that can take my marriage to the next level.

Chapter 2

YOUR SPOUSE NEEDS TO TRUST YOU

Rachelle and Jordan haven't read any self-help books on relationships, so they aren't yet at your level. They don't have to be, because they're five years old. They're just playing on the playground at recess having a great time learning how relationships function in the real world. Rachelle asks Jordan to play with her on the seesaw, and Jordan agrees. So far, so good.

At first, they have a very enjoyable time playing with each other, but just as Rachelle's full weight rests on the ground and little Jordan is high in the air, one of Rachelle's friends calls out to her, "Rachelle, let's go inside. The teacher brought cupcakes!" As all the little children are running inside, Rachelle has a choice to make — how to dismount. Sure, she could wait until they were both in a position to easily get off of the seesaw, but that might take too much time. She decides Jordan can handle getting off on his own and she hops off the seat, leaving Jordan in for a four-foot, bottom-busting, relationship let-down.

The next time Rachelle asks Jordan to play on the seesaw, or any other playground equipment that requires *trust,* Jordan is unlikely to say yes. That's life, and that's where many couples find themselves when they walk into my office. But for them, the stakes are much greater than scrapes and bruises on the recess playground. Their moments of "free-fall" are moments of deception, unfaithfulness, or betrayal. And in those moments, the relationship hangs in the balance.

If Satan could reach into his bag of tricks and take out his favorite blindfold—the one he uses the most to sabotage couples and keep them from seeing the reality in their relationships—I believe it would be this one. Satan desperately wants to keep you from seeing your spouse's need to trust you. This is the primary way he wrecks marriages. And if you're thinking right now, "*We don't have trust problems.*"—beware. You're on the top of Satan's hit list.

The power of this axiom in life cannot be diminished: the more intimate the relationship, the more trust is required. And, the more trust is required, the more devastating trust breaches will be. You must understand this about your spouse: for the rest of your married life, your husband or wife will *always* be learning things along the way about your trustworthiness. Can he or she be safe with you? Can they risk with you? Will you support them when they are most open and vulnerable? These questions will determine whether or not it's *safe* to be married to you.

THE PRINCIPLE OF
INDIVIDUAL RESPONSIBILTY
AND SHARED OWNERSHIP

At the heart of any cooperative relationship is the realization that each individual has responsibility. Each has their own part to play in the relationship. However, the final product of that individual responsibility will be owned by all the invested partners.

Consider a little-league baseball team. Each of these young athletes has an individual responsibility. One must pitch, another must catch, others guard their bases... you get the idea. However, the team as a whole must own the win or the loss.

Marriage, like any cooperative endeavor, requires both individuals to engage actively in playing their part. Just as a little-leaguer that doesn't guard his assigned base causes the whole team to lose the game, a spouse who fails to do what God has assigned him or her to do creates pain for the other. The closer the relationship, the less you have the ability to insulate the other person from the fallout of your failure. This is what Rachelle and Jordan learned on the playground. In order to make the seesaw work, you need two willing parties. Each must support the other person at pivotal moments. If one fails, the other pays.

Here's the challenge: the day you married your mate, you entered into the most extreme shared ownership relationship of your life. In this relationship, you and your spouse each have your own individual responsibilities, but the end product belongs equally to both of you. You and your spouse are both *depending* on each other to hold up your end of the bargain—to live responsibly with each other in a way that produces results that are in the best interest of you both.

Normal people don't start out their relationship with the intent to break each other's trust. I'll grant that there are some evil people out there, but if you take them out of the mix, I believe that people enter into relationships intending to be trustworthy. The problem is that those intentions don't always materialize. For many couples, trust breakages will spell the beginning of the end. You *need* to understand how this happens.

It's A Familiar Story...

Kyle and Elizabeth can't stop fighting about his job. Kyle is the leader of a very successful national sales team, and travels three days a week with his staff. Kyle loves his work, and is very successful at what he does. Everyone on his team looks up to him, and he continually earns the accolades of his contemporaries. When Kyle thinks about his job, he has very positive feelings and a sense of pride. Unfortunately, when Elizabeth thinks about her husband's job she becomes very upset. Elizabeth has noticed that Kyle's company continues to hire very attractive women on their sales force. When she thinks of her husband traveling in the company of these other women—attending the same meetings, riding in the same cars, and staying in the same hotels, she panics.

Elizabeth has explained to Kyle in no uncertain terms that she is not comfortable with his job. She feels that perhaps it's time for Kyle to consider traveling less.

"Maybe you should consider working a desk job at the home office," she would say to him.

Kyle would become irate and accuse her of being controlling, demanding, and incurably jealous.

"The real problem is that you don't trust me!" he would shout at her before storming out of the house.

The more Kyle and Elizabeth tried to work through the issue, the more angry they would become at each other. Elizabeth could not understand why her husband could not respect her feelings about his job, and Kyle could not understand why his wife seemed insistent on controlling his life.

Then Kyle was called away on a business trip that changed everything. He and Elizabeth had fought the night previous about the fact that he was going to be traveling in a group with a woman that Elizabeth was very threatened by—a woman named Jenny. Jenny had allowed the lines of appropriate business conduct to be blurred several times. She was a little too "comfortable" with Kyle, and Elizabeth was very aware. As was their pattern, Elizabeth told Kyle how upset she was that he was going to be traveling in the same group with this other woman, and Kyle told Elizabeth she didn't have a reason to be upset and she should "get over it." They fought until they were tired, and finally went to sleep.

As Kyle was leaving the house for the airport the next morning, he heard his wife call out to him as he walked out the door.

"Kyle, promise me one thing!" she yelled.

"What?" he responded.

"Please don't be *alone* with her on this trip. I'll feel better if you make sure that there are always other people around. Promise?"

"Okay, I promise."

And he left, fully intending to stand by his commitment. The flight was uneventful, but when he arrived at the airport, he found out that his rental vehicle was unavailable. Apparently there was a mix-up with his reservation. He prepared to wait for an hour for another car to be secured, when suddenly Jenny appeared with a smile and asked, "Need a ride, stranger?"

Instinctively, Kyle knew this moment was important. He had promised his wife that he wouldn't be alone with Jenny, and yet he had the opportunity to avoid sitting around the airport for an hour waiting for a car.

"Sure, thanks." Kyle said.

Riding in the car with Jenny, Kyle felt liberated. His wife had tried to control him, and he had refused to be manipulated. But before he could celebrate too much, he received a text message from his wife.

Hey, sweetheart. I'm sorry about our fight last night. I hope you had a good flight. What are you doing right now?

Something about Elizabeth's direct question caused Kyle to break out into a sweat. He knew he couldn't tell her that he was alone in a car with Jenny. If he did that, Elizabeth would be angry at him for no-telling how long, and he might really be forced to think about changing his job habits. *He had promised*, after all.

Just headed out to the meeting. Hope you have a great day. See you when I get home tomorrow. Love you.

There. He thought. *I didn't lie, and the apocalypse was successfully avoided.*

Unfortunately for Kyle, Elizabeth texted right back with a very perceptive question.

You're not texting and driving are you? Did you get a ride? Are you with someone?

Now Kyle was really backed against a wall. He knew that he had to answer this direct question. Either he would answer it honestly and World War III would ensue, or he would creatively alter the truth a bit. He went with the second approach.

I got a ride with one of the guys.

It's not a lie, Kyle thought, *After all, I think of Jenny as "one of the guys." If Elizabeth could just understand that, we wouldn't be having these stupid fights anyway.*

"Everything okay?" Jenny asked.

"Oh, sure," Kyle answered, "Just normal marriage stuff... you know."

"Your wife giving you a hard time?"

"Not really, we just don't see eye to eye about work stuff..."

Kyle continued on. He hadn't expected to tell Jenny anything about his home life or his marriage. He was surprised to hear himself telling Jenny details about his frustration with Elizabeth. But Jenny turned out to be a great listener, and by the time Kyle was through talking, he truly believed that Jenny understood where he was coming from. *Now, if only Elizabeth could be as reasonable as Jenny,* he thought.

About ten minutes away from their final destination, Jenny pulled into an empty parking lot to check her makeup and give Kyle a chance to put on his suit coat. Jenny quickly grabbed the coat from the back seat and held it up for Kyle to slip into. Then, straightening his tie, she said to him, "I think your wife just doesn't know a good thing when she has it." In that moment, Kyle realized he was hooked. That was the moment that began an affair that would eventually end Kyle and Elizabeth's marriage.

Shortly after Elizabeth left Kyle for good, he came to see me to try to make sense of his situation.

"I don't understand, Pastor," he said, "I know all the right things… I knew then I shouldn't be 'fooling around' with another woman. I fully expected I would always be loyal to my wife. I've even talked friends out of cheating on their spouses. I never thought I was capable of making a mistake like this. How did this happen?"

What do you think? How did it happen? And when do you think that Kyle started breaking Elizabeth's trust? Did he first break her trust when he decided to sleep with another woman? Or, was it earlier—perhaps when he let this other woman flirt with him, and when he flirted back? How about earlier still, when he lied to his wife about whom he was with? I would like to propose to you that it started even before that. Kyle's journey of trust breakage followed a very predictable route… one that many couples travel. I'd like to help you see the wrong turns Kyle made, so that you can avoid ending up at the same destination.

FIRST WRONG TURN: KYLE STOPPED HEARING HIS WIFE

Imagine you are at the hospital for a surgical procedure. Prepped and gowned you are wheeled into the operating room—a very scary place to be. The anesthesiologist activates the IV that will put you to sleep and places the oxygen mask on your face. Now imagine halfway through the operation that you wake up and feel *everything*. You're in intense pain, so you start screaming at the surgeon in order to get him to do something. You use choice words that usually do not reside in your vocabulary. You insult his alma mater, his manhood, and his mother. Your voice reaches a decibel level thought only to be achievable by jet aircraft or space shuttle launches. You're desperate, and it's only getting worse.

Now imagine the surgeon looks over at you and says, "I don't think you're really awake."

Predictably, you respond with more anger... more harsh words... more desperation. Then, holding your spleen in his hands, the doctor answers, "My therapist told me never to respond to someone who speaks to me in anger. So I'm going to take a step back and we'll take a time out here. I'll let you cool off so you can speak to me kindly, and when you're ready to communicate in a gracious way, I'll be happy to come back and resume the conversation. Besides, I think you're being unreasonable here. I'm doing a fine job at being your surgeon, and you're just trying to cause problems."

I just described the average marital fight for you. Usually the fight starts because one or both people are upset about something. *Something hurts.* But when the person that's hurting finally says something, they don't do it very skillfully, and the other person isn't ready to hear it. Then, the argument starts. Just as the surgeon and the patient see each other as unreasonable, marital arguments start because both spouses feel the other is being unreasonable about the issue. Here's a shocking revelation: they're right.

Dealing With Your Unreasonable Spouse

You heard me correctly. There will be moments in your relationship when your spouse will do or say something completely unreasonable. But don't be surprised by that… it's part of life. Doctors, paramedics, midwives, dentists… they'll all tell you the same thing: that people in pain often become unreasonable and difficult. The key is for you to understand how to get to the bottom of the unreasonableness. *Underneath every unreasonable reaction is a reasonable pain or fear.* This is key. If your spouse does or says something that seems supremely unreasonable, you must dig beneath the *content* of the issue and their reaction to it, and get to the *fear or pain.*

Elizabeth can definitely relate to that "surgeon and patient" dynamic we spoke of a moment ago. Elizabeth feels very frightened about what might happen if her husband were to become involved with a co-worker. Kyle knows that she becomes upset about this, but isn't willing to hear about her fear and do something about it. After all, Kyle has a dozen reasons why Elizabeth's negative reaction to his work situation is unreasonable. He feels this gives him license to ignore her poorly chosen words. *She's just being paranoid and jealous as usual,* thinks Kyle. *Besides, if she wants to talk things over, she ought to find a better way to talk to me—a more respectful way.*

Just as the surgeon says, "I don't think you're really awake," Kyle says, "I don't think you have a right to feel the pain you're feeling." That is a message that will *always* take a simple fight and transform it into all-out nuclear warfare.

How To Start Hearing Your Spouse

We've already said that underneath every unreasonable reaction is a reasonable pain or fear. So let's talk about what that looks like in terms of Kyle and Elizabeth. In order to truly see their dynamic, we'll go back to the night Kyle was packing for his trip. As Kyle packed, Elizabeth talked. Kyle was used to tuning out Elizabeth's sarcastic jabs about his business trips, but it was getting harder to ignore.

Elizabeth: You taking your grey suit?

Kyle: Yes.

Elizabeth: Hmm... you never wear that suit for me. Guess it pays to work with you.

Kyle: [*silence*]

Elizabeth: Who's going on this trip anyhow?

    Kyle: The regular group.

Elizabeth: You say that like I'm supposed to know whose in your *little group* (mockingly).

    Kyle: Bob, Patricia, Helen, and Jenny.

Elizabeth: Well, well, Jenny shows up on the list again. You guys are getting to be regular traveling buddies, huh?

    Kyle: What are you getting at?

Elizabeth: You know what I'm getting at. Why can't your job send you on trips with just guys? Why do they have to keep sending you out with these little blonde beauty queens? What are they trying to do? Seems like your company is out to wreck marriages.

By now, Kyle has heard enough. If we were to play this scenario forward as it actually happened, you'd see Kyle giving Elizabeth a piece of his mind—telling her about all the ways in which she was being suspicious, jealous, ungrateful, disrespectful, and so on. As you've read this dialogue, perhaps even you have been keeping track of Elizabeth's unreasonable comments. But, as we said, unreasonable is to be expected when a person is in pain.

What Kyle must learn is how to get underneath the unreasonableness.

I'm going to share with you the same key I would have liked to share with Kyle—the key to hearing your spouse. You can do this with one simple question: *"What bothers you so much about that?"*

Let's break back into the dialogue between Kyle and Elizabeth. Think about how this conversation might have gone if Kyle decided he was on a mission to hear and understand Elizabeth's pain.

Elizabeth: You know what I'm getting at. Why can't your job send you on trips with just guys? Why do they have to keep sending you out with these little blonde beauty queens—what are they trying to do? Seems like your company is out to wreck marriages.

Kyle: What bothers you so much about this? I know you're bothered by my business travel, and I really want to understand how it makes you feel.

Elizabeth: I've been telling you how it makes me feel! I don't think it's right for your company to be sending you on trips with all these young, attractive girls.

Elizabeth is still in protective mode because she doesn't really think that Kyle can understand her pain and be there for her. She's been on the "operating table" for a while, and it will take a bit for her to truly trust that Kyle can hear her.

> *Kyle*: Okay, but for a minute can you tell me what bothers you so much about me going on these trips?

Kyle is on a mission, and he didn't get sidetracked by Elizabeth's comments about his company. Now, Elizabeth is actually having to think through what she's feeling. Her response is huge.

> *Elizabeth*: What bothers me so much is that I'm scared I may lose you. These girls you travel with… I've seen how beautiful they are. I can't compete with that. I know you're a good man and that you would never cheat on purpose, but I can't help but wonder about what you might be tempted to do if the right situation came along. Besides, because I can't be there, I feel even more scared because when I think these things, you're gone and then I'm scared and alone.

This is what Kyle lost when he quit hearing his spouse. He lost the ability to know that his wife was feeling scared and alone. The hours Kyle and Elizabeth spent arguing about whether or not his company was "bad" for sending him out on these trips, and the hours they spent arguing about whether or not Elizabeth was jealous and vindictive — **they were all a supreme waste of time**. These issues were the symptoms not the illness. Elizabeth was scared and alone. When you're tremendously frightened and isolated, everything you say is colored by that emotional experience. This is what Kyle fails to realize. All the things he's hearing from his wife that put him in a tailspin of anger and frustration are shaped by Elizabeth's experience of emotional danger. If Kyle will understand and deal with that danger, Elizabeth is likely to behave very differently.

Here's the other key: assuming Kyle is a good person (and he is), if he finds a way to understand Elizabeth's true feelings, he is *far more likely to make personal changes himself,* because he'll have the opportunity to change with dignity.

Change With Dignity

These three words— "change with dignity"—are the hallmark of my work with couples. I do not believe that people are shamed into productive change. I believe that most of us make changes when we can do so with dignity. So it's highly unlikely that Kyle is going to evaluate his work habits and consider possible changes simply because his wife is upset. Even if he made changes just "to keep the peace" he would resent having to make them, and would quickly be dealing with new problems. Kyle's one chance to make productive changes in his life happens when he chooses to hear and understand what his wife is going through.

When you excavate beneath the unreasonable reaction and get to the pain or fear that is motivating it, you will have the opportunity to witness something about your spouse that few will get the privilege of seeing. You will see their most basic *needs*. Most of us don't share these with our spouse because we're used to projecting a "put-together" image. For many of us, part of living in a demanding world is finding a way to avoid sharing our deepest needs. But this is a part of marriage that cannot be averted. You can't be there for your spouse and they can't be there for you until there is a moment where the *real needs* are being put on the table. Needs like the ones you'll read about in the next six chapters.

I believe you're a person who wants to have success in your marriage. I get that from the fact that you're actually taking some of your valuable time to read this book. That being the case, I expect that you have a heart to do the right thing by your spouse. That might even mean making some changes in your life. My point is that you will likely change when you can do so with dignity, and you'll not have that opportunity unless you ask the questions necessary to get to the heart of your spouse's deepest needs.

Once you understand those needs, your desire to do the right thing will kick in, and you can begin the journey necessary to provide safety for your spouse in those areas. I believe that if Kyle had simply learned to follow this process, he could have enjoyed the rest of his life with the woman he loved, instead of losing her.

SECOND WRONG TURN: KYLE STOPPED BEING HONEST WITH HIS WIFE

Kyle knew *what* caused his wife pain—his job. As a result, he knew that whenever the issue came up, Elizabeth was going to become desperate and irate. Kyle didn't like it when his wife was desperate and irate, and as a result, he developed a comfort level with "adjusting" the truth a bit to keep harmony and peace in the marriage. Kyle allowed himself to even eventually believe that his creative treatment of the truth was beneficial for his wife and kids. *I'm keeping Elizabeth from freaking out… and that's a good thing,* he thought.

But deception of any kind is poison in a marriage relationship. Here's why: God intended marriage to be an enterprise of "oneness." We see that truth emphasized when God explains the purpose and plan of marriage in Genesis 2:24, and again when Jesus reiterates the plan in Matthew 19:5-6. So if God's agenda for marriage is oneness, you can be guaranteed that Satan's agenda for your marriage is "separate-ness." And that is exactly what deception does to your relationship. The truth unites you and your spouse. The truth is something you have in common. It's not "your truth" and "her truth," or "your truth" and "his truth." There is only truth. But if deception enters your marriage, you each have your own "truth"—your *separate* "truth."

Why Is Honesty Such a Big Deal?

You benefit from something your spouse will never

have—you always know what you're thinking. Presumably, you always know what you're doing and what you have done. Much of that is a mystery to your spouse. They will often have only one thing to go on—*what you say*. Our words have more power than most of us will ever realize. Since your spouse cannot know what you are thinking, and since they cannot always know what you are doing, they are listening to what you say. Your words have power. If they are true, your spouse is *learning to trust you*. If your words are false, your spouse is learning *not to trust you*. It's as simple as that.

What are you teaching your spouse? They have a *need to trust* that will either be reinforced by your words, or demolished by them. You *must be honest*. You <u>must be</u>. Marriages are resilient. My work with couples has taught me time and again that couples can survive difficulty, learn to conquer it, and thrive by God's grace. However, this will *never happen* in a culture of dishonesty.

When dishonesty enters your marriage relationship, Satan is getting what he wants. He wants to end the trust in your marriage. He wants husbands and wives to be deceptive and suspicious. Tell Satan to take a hike, and then tell the truth—about everything. Be diligent not to get comfortable with seemingly harmless dishonesty like "fibs" or "white lies." Deception is like a drug... you'll need a bigger "fix" next time, and the bigger the deception, the more you are at risk for making a huge wrong turn in the relationship... just ask Kyle.

Think about this: the moment Kyle became comfortable not telling his wife the whole truth, he was perfectly positioned for Satan to tempt him with an affair. In John 3:19, Jesus tells us that "darkness" has a way of accommodating "evil deeds." Kyle may not realize it, but every time he tells Elizabeth something that's not true, he creates a little more darkness in his relationship. By the time the lights completely go out, Kyle becomes one of Satan's easiest targets.

THIRD WRONG TURN: KYLE STOPPED BEING FAITHFUL TO HIS WIFE

There is a reason we're comparing Kyle's life decisions with wrong turns. If you take a wrong turn early on in an extended road trip, it's very likely you will find yourself very far from your intended destination at the end of your journey. Just so, Kyle's wrong decisions led him to a destination he would never have envisioned for himself. If you had told Kyle on his wedding day that he would eventually sleep with another woman and break his wife's heart, Kyle would likely have been filled with righteous indignation. That was something he would *never do*. But his own actions betrayed his intentions.

Kyle knew all the right things. He had sat through church services when the preacher talked about the importance of being faithful to your spouse. He had encouraged others to do the right thing. He even had the Bible verse that talks about this memorized.

Hebrews 13:4 (NLT)
⁴ Give honor to marriage, and remain faithful to one another in marriage. God will surely judge people who are immoral and those who commit adultery.

Like most of us, Kyle was very aware of the fact that God expected him to be faithful to his spouse and commit his romantic attention to Elizabeth only. But none of these realizations kept Kyle from entering into an affair. That's why he was so disheartened and confused when he came to see me. That's why his struggle to find an answer for his bad behavior was so deep. What I'm about to share with you could be the key to making sure you don't follow Kyle's footsteps and make a very painful mistake.

THE SURPRISING ORDER OF TRUST

By looking at the three "wrong turns" Kyle made, we have identified three major keys to being trustworthy with your spouse: hearing, being honest, and being faithful. The secret to understanding trust is to realize that many of us get the order of those keys backwards. Kyle didn't break trust the first time by cheating on Elizabeth. He first broke her trust by choosing not to hear and understand her pain. It was that choice—the choice not to hear—that created conflict in the relationship and caused Kyle to be deceptive and create a "separate truth." And it was living in a world of "separate truth" that positioned Kyle to be at risk for an affair.

Like many of us, Kyle spent his time as a husband watching and waiting for Satan to burst through the front door of his marriage and try to get him to be unfaithful or dishonest. But Satan likes to sneak in through the back door, and when he does, he starts by robbing our relationship of understanding. He knows that if he can get a person to quit hearing their spouse, he is much more likely to get them to be dishonest, and ultimately, unfaithful.

How does this work? Simple. First we become unable to "hear" each other. That basically means that we can't communicate. When tough issues or problems surface, we can't process them in an effective way, so major conflict results. After we experience this pattern, we eventually come to the belief that we *can't* communicate about what's *really happening*. Reality is too difficult on the relationship, so we begin to color the truth—so as not to make waves. It's surprising how much conflict we're able to avoid this way. Then we become experts at shaping the truth so our spouse won't react badly, and the deception drug begins to deaden the pain of a relationship that is dying on the inside. Once deception has firmly taken root and is growing (in its characteristic weed-like fashion), Satan merely needs to find the right time, place, and circumstance to tempt you in order to take you down. It all starts with something that seems simple, but may be the most important quality of a marriageable person—the ability to "hear."

When Jesus was approached by the Pharisees about the issue of divorce in Matthew 19, Jesus said that divorce was allowed by Moses only as a "concession" because of the people's "hard hearts." You may be interested to know that this condition—the condition of a hard heart—is characterized in Scripture as being the result of being unable to "see" and "hear."

Matthew 13:15a (NLT)
15 For the hearts of these people are hardened,
and their ears cannot hear,
and they have closed their eyes—
so their eyes cannot see,
and their ears cannot hear,
and their hearts cannot understand...

The enemy of trust in a marriage is a hard heart. When we become unable to see the other person's experience, hear them out and understand their fear or pain, we are most at risk of not living up to the high calling of marriage.

The Trustworthy Heart

So, you have a choice to make. The Bible tells us that having a hard heart puts your marriage on a divorce trajectory. So imagine what kind of power you could bring to your marriage by softening your heart. How do you do that? First, you need to make the choice to really open your eyes and ears so that you can understand what your spouse is feeling. Then, you need to make the choice to be honest—even when it means "rocking the boat." The fact that you choose to tell the truth even when you know it won't be popular will help your spouse feel confident that you're not in the business of hiding things. Finally, fix your romantic attention on your spouse. It belongs to them.

Dear God,

I ask You to help me as I try to inspire my spouse to trust me. I know You created each of us with a need for safety, and I want to make my spouse feel completely safe with me. Please help me to hear my spouse—help me to understand their feelings. Help me to remember to always be honest… never to treat the truth as if it were secondary to convenience. Then, Lord, help me to not only be faithful, but to inspire my spouse to believe I am faithful. Help me to teach them through my words and actions that my heart belongs to them.

Chapter 3

YOUR SPOUSE NEEDS YOU TO BE THERE FOR THEM

Travis and Dawn are a couple in their late twenties just trying to survive the toddlerhood of their two precious children. Don't get me wrong, they love being parents, but they had no idea how much work it would be. Years earlier they had been a happy-go-lucky dating couple. Their biggest problem was figuring out which movie to see and which restaurant to visit afterward. Now they have bigger problems... car seats, baby gates, teething, rashes, pink eye... life is more challenging now than they ever could have imagined.

Usually Travis is an involved and caring parent. He loves Dawn and truly wants to honor God by being a great husband. Sometimes, however, he's a little insensitive to Dawn's plight as a stay-at-home mom. Dawn never has a grown-up to talk to. When the kids chew on something they're not supposed to, or flush something big enough to clog the pipes, she needs to talk to somebody about it—somebody older than two.

Dawn was having one of those days. Everything had gone wrong. It started when the UPS guy came when she was in the shower. His knocking woke up the kids, and she had to answer the door with a kid in each arm, shampoo in her hair, and her robe on backwards. Later, one of the kids started throwing up and she had to take him to the pediatrician. The doctor prescribed a medication that—of course—would not be ready until later, making it necessary that she get out of the house later in the day.

After all of this fun, Dawn's sister called to gripe about her husband. Dawn was used to this, but this wasn't the day for it. Dawn politely asked her sister if they could talk about it another time, and her sister became angry with her. *Just great,* she thought. *That's all I need, one more fire to put out later.*

At about three o'clock, Dawn started to feel herself getting nauseated. *I can't do this,* she thought. *I can't be sick and take care of sick kids. I need Travis.*

Dawn picked up the phone and dialed Travis. No answer. *He might be on a service call,* she thought. *I'll wait a bit.* She called twenty minutes later. No answer again. By the time Travis came home—5:30 p.m.—Dawn was in a slightly-less-than-charitable mood. Travis came home and Dawn tried her best to tell him the events of her day in sequential order. As Dawn talked, Travis muttered the usual listening cues, the "uh-huh's," "um-hmms," and so forth, but Dawn had the distinct feeling he wasn't listening.

As Dawn talked, Travis walked to the bedroom to change out of his work uniform. She talked while he checked his email and text messages. By the time she got to the fact that she wasn't feeling well, he had positioned himself on the couch in front of the TV set. He looked up at Dawn and said, "Wow. I bet you're glad this day is over. Let me know if you need me to get you anything." Then Travis turned on the TV and began watching his favorite show.

Travis is a good guy, but he doesn't understand that his marriage is on its way to being in real trouble. Travis' behavior was sending Dawn a very clear message: "This is your problem. I guess I'll help if you need me, but don't expect me to save the day. Don't expect me to be your 'knight in shining armor.' Don't expect me to be there for you." *Travis doesn't understand how much Dawn is counting on him.* Dawn's life is full of challenges and problems. She wasn't meant to face them alone. When Dawn feels that Travis isn't there for her, she finds herself feeling desperate and abandoned.

When Dawn and Travis came to see me about their marriage difficulties, I did for them what I would like to do for you now. I would like to take you back in time to the moment God instituted his invention of marriage. In a rare moment of recorded self-talk, we have a moment of God's own thinking about why marriage was necessary and how it should function.

Genesis 2:18 (NLT)
18 Then the Lord God said, "It is not good for the man to
be alone. I will make a helper who is just right for him."

I can't think of any scripture passage that more plainly states the purpose of marriage. Remember that during the creation account, God looks on every bit of His masterpiece and pronounces His approval by calling each element "good." Isn't it interesting, then, that in this case—this single case—God pronounces part of His creation "not good." He tells us, "It is not good for the man to be *alone.*"

Think about the power of this insight. God—the Creator of human life—is telling us a fundamental concept about how we were designed to function. He is telling us that we were not meant to live life alone. Additionally, God illustrated His plan for a remedy. Notice, God did not help Adam survive by creating a tribe of individuals to fulfill the "it takes a village" cliché. He didn't intend for Adam to survive by creating multiple women so he could discover satisfaction by experimenting with his sexual urges. No, God created Eve. One woman and one man, one devoted life-long relationship of companionship and support—this was God's design to make something that once was "not good" "good."

For most of us, marriage will be our greatest opportunity to experience companionship, intimacy, and support. However, many marriages fail to accomplish the goal of productive togetherness. When I do couple's coaching, I have the couple fill out forms in advance. Two of the questions I ask are, "Has your spouse always been there for you?" and "Do you believe your spouse will always be there for you?" I have found that the answers to those questions often tell me a great deal of what I need to know about the health of the relationship.

THE DESIGN: BETTER TOGETHER

In Matthew 19, Jesus talks about how marriage was designed to work. He was talking to the ultra-elite of the religious crowd of His day. They positioned themselves against Jesus, because they didn't believe He was God. Ultimately, they wanted to kill Him. For the time present, they were satisfied with trying to discredit Him.

In the United States, we go through an election cycle every couple of years, so we're used to this. The candidate holds a press conference or appears at a public event, and someone from the opposition asks *the question*. You know it's coming. It's a loaded question, full of emotion with ardent supporters on each side of the issue. By answering the question, the candidate will win brownie points with some individuals, and lose support from others. Divide and conquer... that's the competitive strategy.

Jesus was already on record as having said that divorce was only allowable in the case of adultery. But no-fault divorce was popular. There were plenty of religious teachers preaching that a husband could divorce his wife for the silliest of reasons—if she burned dinner for instance, or let her hair down in public, or criticized his mother. The

Pharisees thought that if they caught Jesus in a public place and forced him to state his views on divorce for all to hear that he would lose big time.

> *Matthew 19:3 (NLT)*
> *3 Some Pharisees came and tried to trap him with this question: "Should a man be allowed to divorce his wife for just any reason?"*

If Jesus re-stated that in God's eyes divorce is only acceptable when adultery has taken place, then the crowd would reject Him because it was more convenient for them to believe the easy-divorce guys. If, however, Jesus did the popular thing and agreed that no-fault divorce was okay, then they could accuse Him of changing His stance on the issue.

Here's where the Pharisees underestimated Jesus. Since Jesus is God, and God designed marriage, He wasn't the slightest bit interested in talking to these bozos about how to go about ending a marriage. Now was the time to talk about how to go about making marriage work.

> *Matthew 19:4–6 (NLT)*
> *4 "Haven't you read the Scriptures?" Jesus replied. "They record that from the beginning 'God made them male and female.' 5 And he said, 'This explains why a man leaves his father and mother and is joined to his wife, and the two are united into one.' 6 Since they are no longer two but one, let no one split apart what God has joined together."*

Jesus asks, "Haven't you read the Scriptures?" This question is classic. Jesus is reminding these guys that the design instructions for marriage are plainly spelled out in Genesis. The Pharisees ask how to *handle the failure of a marriage,* but Jesus chooses instead to talk about how to *restore the purpose of a marriage.* I'd like you to pay attention to every word in verses 5 and 6 that refer to the concept of two people "being there" for each other.

> *Matthew 19:5–6 (NLT)*
> *5 And he said, 'This explains why a man leaves his father and mother and is **joined** to his wife, and the two are **united into one.**' 6 Since they are **no longer two** **but one**, **let no one split apart** what **God has joined together**."*
> *[emphasis added]*

Look at all the togetherness in these verses. I love what Jesus is telling the Pharisees here. It's like He's saying, "Guys, why waste time talking about how to get out of a marriage when we could be talking about how to make marriage work?" Think about the power of what Jesus says in verse 6: God has joined you and your spouse together. When a man and woman enter into marriage, God is actually at work doing something in the relationship. He is at work strengthening the glue that holds you and your spouse together.

But if God wants to bring you and your spouse closer together, you can bet that Satan's agenda is to pull you apart. Satan wants to divide and conquer. This has been his strategy all along. After all, the main message Satan gave to Eve in the Garden of Eden was, "You don't need God on your team. He's holding you back. Strike out on your own. You're better off going solo." Things haven't changed much. He's still trying to convince people they are better off on their own.

In your married life, you will have to decide between these two ideas. God has stated that it's not good for you to do life alone. You need him, and you need your spouse. God created you for healthy dependency. When your marriage is working as God intended, you and your spouse will be *better together* than alone. Satan knows that, so he will try to thin you from the herd. He will try to convince you that there's more benefit to being self-sufficient. In our culture today, *Satan is very good at convincing married people to live like single people.* Be aware, it doesn't work.

THE LIFELINE

If you want to experience marriage that lives up to God's design, and if you want to bring purpose and fulfillment to your marriage, it's important to understand that God designed your relationship to be an enterprise of togetherness. God wants you and your spouse to function as partners. Your spouse needs your help.

Genesis 2:18 (NLT)
18 Then the Lord God said, "It is not good for the man to be alone. I will make a helper who is just right for him."

When God said He would make a "helper who is just right" for Adam, the word rendered "helper" means more than just a companion. Companionship is definitely implied, but the word helper here also means a support system. It means someone that surrounds you with assistance. God created marriage to be a partnership. Both individuals are to be invested in each other's success. Husbands and wives are to be willing to put each other's needs first, and if either is in danger the other is to be a lifeline.

I'm relatively afraid of heights, so I've always been impressed by people who are willing to make a living building high rise apartments, washing windows on sky-scrapers, or repairing television or radio towers. These people's capacity to deal with the danger of falling is incredible to me. However, one thing you'll notice about all of these individuals is that they all wear some sort of *lifeline* or fall protection. They all have some sort of safety system to minimize the danger of their everyday work.

Emotionally speaking, we all have to cope with the potential of frightening situations. Just as the high-wire worker double checks to make sure his harness will protect him from accidental falls, your spouse double-checks to see if you are there for them. They know their life is full of potential for danger. Just doing everyday life means taking risks and facing overwhelming challenges. They need to know you will be there no matter what happens. Your presence makes the danger much less intimidating.

Years ago, a brilliant psychologist by the name of Mary Ainsworth was studying the bonds between mothers and infants, and how the health and strength of that bond impacted the child's behavior. Her observation tells us a lot about this lifeline concept. As the children she studied entered the typical exploration stage of toddlerhood, they often developed a comfort level with venturing away from the mother and looking for things to do and objects to play with, even in unfamiliar surroundings.

But, from time to time, the small child would look back at his mom to make sure she was still there. Sometimes the child would even take a break from exploration and return to his mother for a while. After enjoying some close contact with mom, the child would return to his expedition, looking for cool stuff to do.

From childhood, we have each had a need for a "lifeline." Just as the infants in Ainsworth's studies needed to be able to glance over their shoulder and know that "mom was still there," we, as adults, need that sense of security that comes from the assurance that our spouse will always be there for us. When we are certain of our spouse's willingness to be a support system for us, we can take on life's challenges with much more confidence, despite the risks.

Psalm 23 gives us some insight to the importance of a lifeline.

Psalm 23:4 (NIV)
4 Even though I walk
through the darkest valley,
I will fear no evil,
for you are with me;
your rod and your staff,
they comfort me.

King David speaks of the "darkest valley" in this Psalm. Most of us have had "darkest valley" moments. When we experience the greatest challenges of our life, the danger seems overwhelming. The risk is almost too much for us. In those moments, we long for a safety net—some way to know that things will be alright.

Notice that David did not say:

Even though I walk through the darkest valley, I will fear no evil *because I will analyze the situation and determine the best way to cope.*

Even though I walk through the darkest valley, I will fear no evil *because I must be strong and self-sufficient — else I will prove my own weakness.*
Even though I walk through the darkest valley, I will fear no evil *because it's best to ignore danger, and pretend nothing's wrong.*

Instead, David says:

"Even though I walk through the darkest valley, I

will fear no evil,
   for you are with me; your rod and your staff, they comfort me."

David is saying, "God, You are my lifeline." When I face difficult, dangerous, frightening circumstances, I look for You. You are always there, and I know that I can face the danger when You are with me.

So you might be thinking, "Okay, Jonathan, so is my spouse supposed to depend on me, or on God?" The answer is *yes.* As God-followers, we should depend on God first in all of our relationships. His presence is the first line of defense for all the fearful situations we experience in life. However, God has called you to be an *additional presence*—an *additional lifeline*—that provides even more safety for your spouse in moments of difficulty.

Through the years, preachers have often told the story of a little boy who was frightened one night by a terrible storm. Understanding his fear, the boy's mother held him in her arms and reminded him that everything would be okay.

"God will take care of us," she said, hoping this would calm her son's trembling.

Each time she tried to leave his room, he would call out to her, "Mom—don't leave, I'm scared!"

Eventually, his mom said, "Son, you will be alright. It's time for you to go to sleep now. God will take care of you. Good night."

At this, the little boy reached out and grabbed his mother by the waist refusing to let her go. He shouted as he held her tightly, "I know God will take care of me, but I need God with skin on!"

> *Ephesians 5:1–2 (NLT)*
> ***Imitate God***, *therefore, in everything you do, because you are his dear children. 2* ***Live a life filled with love, following the example of Christ***. *He loved us and offered himself as a sacrifice for us, a pleasing aroma to God.* *[emphasis added]*

In our relationship with our spouse, God has called us to be an imitator of Him. When we truly live up to God's calling in our lives, *we are a flesh and blood extension of God's presence in our spouse's life — "God with skin on."* In moments of difficulty and fear, God wants you to be an extension of His love that your spouse can see, hear, touch, and hold. Don't sell short the power of your presence. You are the most tangible lifeline your spouse can access. Your spouse's confidence in many ways hinges on their ability to *access* you.

Our culture has convinced many of us that to *need a lifeline*—to be dependent on another person for emotional safety and stability—is a sign of weakness. Our culture promotes the idea that you need to realize that you don't "need" anyone. Self-sufficiency is presented as the way to be happy and secure. But the Bible and scholarly research agree — this just isn't so.

Recent research by Psychologist Brooke Feeney indicates that the more healthily dependent we are in close relationships, the more we are courageous to meet challenges and make decisions individually. It may sound strange at first, but think of it this way: If a high-rise construction worker insists on wearing a safety harness when going to work, it doesn't mean he lacks courage. In fact, *he's much more likely to be courageous and take risks when he's wearing the harness.* The fact that he insists on wearing the lifeline just means that he has a healthy respect for the danger he will encounter. *His need for a support system is a healthy need, not a sign of weakness.*

What does all this mean? It means that admitting you need your spouse *doesn't* mean you're weak. And, by the same token, your spouse is not weak for needing you. God designed you to need each other. You are a support system — you are a lifeline. Please don't underestimate the beauty and importance of this responsibility. You are God's representative of love to your spouse.

When you read the book of Psalms and see verse after verse about how God is a refuge and a solace — a safe place to run to — remember that God has called you to provide the same emotional safety for your spouse.

TAKING YOUR SPOUSE SERIOUSLY

I'm very aware that as I write this book, I'm using terms that seem more emotional than practical. Maybe you find it a bit hard to take me seriously when I introduce ideas like "emotional danger." I'm a guy, and in a guy's world we don't talk about emotional things very often because they feel like unnecessary drama. Please understand that I'm not talking about emotional danger and emotional safety for the sake of additionally dramatizing what you and your spouse go through. I'm trying to help you understand what motivates our relationships to struggle.

God built us as emotional beings. When we experience emotional safety, our lives have the greatest potential to be productive and healthy. When our emotional life is full of danger, we simply can't function as God intended. This being the case, one of the most important parts of being a lifeline for your spouse is understanding the danger they face. We talked a little bit about this in the previous chapter.

Remember when we talked about the patient on the operating table that woke up in the middle of surgery? We said that the surgeon *must be willing to understand the patient's pain, even though he can't feel the pain.* This is part of being a lifeline for your spouse. *You can't provide emotional safety for your spouse if you don't understand what feels dangerous to them.* If you ever catch yourself thinking or saying, "I don't know why my spouse is so upset by this—it wouldn't upset me" you are missing this step. Understanding emotional danger in your marriage will frequently involve *understanding pain you don't and probably won't personally feel.*

For instance, imagine a young woman who makes a habit of frequenting bars. Her husband doesn't at all feel comfortable with this habit. She responds by asserting that she is a responsible drinker (whatever that is) and that she hasn't given him any particular reason to believe that she would do something terrible. However, he doesn't view her going to the bars, drinking, and talking with other men as a positive thing in their relationship. For him, this is very scary. What if she meets another man? What if she becomes too intoxicated to exercise good judgment? The "what if's" are debilitating and he tells her that he wishes she would no longer frequent these establishments.

Why is she unlikely to receive his request in the spirit it was made? Because she doesn't feel the pain that he feels. She doesn't feel the danger that he experiences. She's much more likely to argue with him or accuse him of not trusting her than to pay attention to the most important message: "Your spouse is in danger. You are his lifeline. Pay attention!" When our spouse tries to tell us what creates danger for them — *especially if it's something we do or don't do* — it can be very hard for us to hear. But make no mistake about it, your spouse is standing on the ledge. They are in a moment of personal danger. Something is happening that causes them pain. They are trying to find out if you'll be there for them.

When this happens, there are three major thought patterns you *must avoid*. These three mantras will eat away at the safety in your relationship and leave both of you alone and hurting.

1. I don't feel it, so I shouldn't have to deal with it.

When Wendy and I were first married, we met a young couple with which we had much in common. They were also newlyweds and we enjoyed spending time together. One of the things that we learned, though, was that this couple had argued for some time about his car magazines. At the time, I was in the car repair industry, as was this young man, and many of my friends subscribed to these publications. There was information about tuning sports cars in these magazines, but there were also quite a few pictures of scantily clad women decorating the pages as well.

This young man's wife was upset — and rightfully so — about his insistence on "reading" these magazines, and asked him to consider how it made her feel. She wanted him to stop buying the magazines. But *he didn't feel the way she felt*. He felt that he didn't buy the magazines to stare at the pictures. In his mind, the magazines were research for his intended field of work. Because he didn't feel the way she felt, he simply ignored her requests and continued his hurtful behavior. He was basically saying to her, "I'll only be your lifeline if *I can see the danger*. If you can't prove you're in danger, I won't be your lifeline." It was this dynamic that characterized the first years of this couples' marriage. It's no wonder, then, that they divorced very early on.

We've already said that Satan is the enemy of productive relationships. One of his primary weapons against marriage is the weapon of pride. Satan convinces us to stand up for our rights and desires before considering our spouse's. Sometimes we can begin to adopt a stance of, "If I can't feel it, can't understand it, don't believe it, or don't want to hear it, I can just ignore it." There's a very simple reason why we tend to fall into this negative thought pattern. When I decide that my feelings and desires trump those of my spouse, it puts *me first.*

> *Ephesians 5:21 (NLT)*
> *21 And further, submit to one another out of reverence for Christ.*

However, our God-given responsibility in marriage is to put the other person first. The above verse is an instruction for husbands and wives. Through the Apostle Paul, God is telling us what our *role* is to be with our spouse. The Greek word rendered "submit" here was a military term, meaning "to rank under." It basically means, "to push your spouse to the front of the line." It means to put your spouse first—to put their wishes and concerns above your own. Why would God ask us to do this? I believe one major reason is this: in order to be the "helper" God wants us to be in our spouse's life, we will need to give honor to their feelings and desires even when we don't hold them in common.

Being a God-honoring spouse means being willing to *understand and engage* what we don't feel. It means being willing to realize that what our spouse feels is *real to them.* It means honoring their experience—understanding that we are different people and we will see things differently. If we can appreciate our spouse's experience without insisting that it mirror our own, we are well on our way to being the lifeline our spouse desperately needs.

2. My spouse is wrong, so my job is to explain why my point of view is right.

One couple I worked with faced a major decision regarding the wife's occupation. She was working very long hours and was away from home a majority of the time. Her income continued to increase, and the family enjoyed the benefit of the extra cash. Her husband, however, felt that the family was suffering from the fact that she was not around. "I wish you would consider taking a job where you would be able to work fewer hours and spend more time at home," he would say, "and then we could be more like a family again."

She didn't have any intention of leaving her job. She felt fulfilled at work, and enjoyed being able to contribute to the family's financial stability. In her mind, the family needed the income she provided. If she worked fewer hours, the family would suffer. In his mind, the family was already suffering from her absence, and could do with a little less income.

When they arrived at my office, they argued about this issue with incredible tenacity. He acted as though his one mission in life was to *convince* her that she should find another job, and that the family would be able to live on less money. She felt that her mission was to *convince* him that they needed her income, and that it would be "insane" for her to leave a job she loved for "no good reason."

This couple was stuck in something I refer to as the "fight to be right." It happens when we come to the belief that we have the "right" perspective on a given situation. Because we come to the belief we are "right," our disagreeing spouse must therefore be "wrong." This being the case, we become excellent debaters. We find a way to articulate our position, and we communicate it over and over again. We tend to accidentally stop listening to the other person. After all, they're wrong anyhow, and we listen increasingly to our own point of view and those who share it.

It's no wonder that as long as we're stuck in the "fight to be right," we can't achieve the goal of "being there for each other." It's impossible. The "fight to be right" is all about winning. We want our viewpoint or feelings to emerge preeminent over our spouse's.

Remember, though, God designed marriage to be a team sport. When marriage functions as God planned, you and your spouse are on the same team. That means if your spouse loses, you lose too.

3. If my spouse would only be more like me...

In the world of psychological research relating to marriage, you won't find many names more prominent than that of John Gottman. His ability to develop assessment tools and experimental environments to study marriage is unparalleled. Dr. Gottman's most heralded achievement was his ability to predict from his research the probability of divorce among the couples he researched with ninety-four percent accuracy.

The single most important predictor of divorce in Dr. Gottman's study was a culture of contempt. Some individuals he studied began behaving as though they were better than their spouse. Their body language, facial expression, tone of voice, interactive style, and word choice indicated a sort of disgust for the other person. Basically, they get to the point that they simply wish their spouse could be *more like them.*

Contempt definitely sounds like a bad deal, but why would it predict divorce? One couple I worked with demonstrated the reason beautifully. In the course of our first session, she revealed that his insistence on having several women "friends" was extremely frightening to her. He would often insist on meeting these women to "hang out," and most of the time she was not invited. He continued throughout the session to explain to me how unreasonable it was for her to insist that he not be with his friends, be they male or female. He wanted her to to "chill out"... *to be more like him.*

I'll never forget when the moment of risk came in the session. I don't know how she found the courage to do it, but she was completely open and vulnerable with him about how his behavior made her feel. "I think I will lose you," she said. "That's what I sit at home and think. I try to keep my mind off it by taking care of the baby and cleaning the house, but in the back of my mind, I keep thinking I will lose you. It's too much for me. I need you to help me feel safe by putting me above your 'friends.'"

As a person who works with a lot of couples, I was absolutely floored by her willingness to risk with him — her willingness to let down her guard and speak to him about her most basic feelings of pain and fear. For many couples, this would be a huge step in the right direction. Unfortunately, he responded not with empathy and understanding, but contempt. "That's your problem," he said, "not mine. Every guy deserves to have friends, and you don't get to pick who my friends are. You definitely don't get to pick when I spend time with them. It sounds to me like this is your personal problem. I don't think I even need to be here."

This is why a culture of contempt is so destructive to marriage relationships. When your spouse is vulnerable with you — when they find a way to expose their deepest feelings to you, you must remember that the danger in that moment is huge for them. They are really risking with you. Being there for your spouse will reduce the danger of the risk. Showing contempt for your spouse will make the situation more emotionally dangerous. This means that if you can find a way to show empathy and understanding, you prove to your spouse that the lifeline is in tact and worth relying on. If you show contempt, you will inspire them to risk less, because the lifeline seems to be gone when they need it most.

THE BOTTOM LINE

Every time your spouse risks with you they are giving you a golden opportunity to be there for them. Every time they become open and vulnerable with you, you have a chance to be their lifeline. Being there in a moment of emotional danger for your spouse is not just a way to develop intimacy, it's a way to imitate God (Eph. 5:1) and to be "God with skin on" for your spouse. *The power of your presence is something your spouse desperately needs.*

Dear God,
I am so thankful that You are always there for me. Some-times I forget that my spouse needs me to be "God with skin on." Sometimes it's hard to be an extension of your love to an imperfect person. Help me to do this in Your strength.

Chapter 4

YOUR SPOUSE NEEDS YOUR COMFORT

"He just dropped me off—right at the door; he didn't say one word. Here I was miscarrying our second child and my husband was nowhere to be found. I was so embarrassed. I was giving the nurses and doctors his cell phone number. 'Please call him; I don't know where he is...I need him,' I said. They kept telling me, 'There's no answer, we'll keep trying.' He was gone."

"How could a loving husband treat me this way? He says I'm the woman he loves, but how can he say he loves me and then leave me? My parents are advising me to leave him. I feel like I should leave him. After all, if he can't be there for me in the middle of a miscarriage, what kind of fool would I be to expect him to be there the next time something bad happens?"

Can you hear the agony in this woman's words? It's unfathomable to her that her husband could be missing in action in a moment when she is experiencing the deepest pain of her life. She knew that this would be difficult for both of them. She had miscarried before. This was the second time. The first time had been almost unbearable for both of them. But they had survived — together. Now she felt completely alone.

I asked her husband what happened. "I panicked." He said. "I didn't know what to do. I dropped her off at the door, fully intending to park the car and run behind her into the emergency room. But as I drove to the parking lot, all the memories and emotions of the last time overwhelmed me. This was the same hospital with the same doctors and nurses. They would say the same thing again. We would go through the same pain again. It was too much for me. I sat in the parking lot crying, pounding the steering wheel with my fists, yelling at God, and wishing the whole thing was a bad dream."

Throughout the evening in the hospital, this precious woman kept thinking the same thoughts. *I can't believe I'm alone. This makes no sense. Why would he abandon me? I'm going to have to go through this all by myself. The only one who will take care of me is me.* That last statement — "the only one who will take care of me is me" — is the one that ripped apart the fabric of this couple's relationship.

I have observed in my work with couples that pain either tends to bring couples together, or push them apart. It is as though pain is a sort of *catalyst* that speeds up the overall dynamic of the relationship. If you and your spouse are moving closer together when traumatic events transpire, the pain of that experience will likely bring you closer faster. If you and your spouse are stagnant or moving apart, pain will create distance in a hurry.

Regardless of your life circumstance, education, background, income, etc., you and your spouse will go through moments of pain and grief. Mark it down — it will happen. In this chapter, we're talking about moments of pain that *neither of you can control.* Life will throw difficult circumstances at you that are not the fault of you or your spouse. How do you survive pain you can't fix? This couple didn't ask for the pain of a miscarriage, and neither individual can do anything to make the situation different. This is pain they can't control, and their marriage depends on how they face it together. In this chapter we'll explore how you and your spouse can be there for each other when you experience these difficult moments.

I know that it's hard to know what to do when you see your spouse going through moments of intense personal difficulty. It can be intimidating. *Often you will be experiencing your own pain simultaneously.* Maybe you can identify with this young man as he sits in his car sobbing over a loss that both he and his wife deeply feel. Maybe you've been in a similar situation. I want to encourage you with this truth: you have what it takes to comfort your spouse. If I could go back in time and speak to him as he sat in his car grieving, I'd share with him three major realizations that would help him know how to comfort his wife through the pain.

REALIZATION #1: THIS MAY INVOLVE ME, BUT IT'S NOT ABOUT ME.

One of the most interesting stories about a married couple in the Bible is found in I Samuel 1. The family described in this passage would have easily made the callback list for a reality TV series. There was one husband and two wives. (That in and of itself spells dysfunction.) But if that wasn't enough, Hannah (the focal point of our story) could not have children. Her husband's other wife, Peninnah, could. In her culture, a woman's worth was highly tied to her ability to have children. It didn't help that Peninnah taunted Hannah about her inability to conceive.

1 Samuel 1:1a, 3a, 4-8 (NLT)
There was a man named Elkanah who lived in Ramah in the region of Zuph in the hill country of Ephraim…
3 Each year Elkanah would travel to Shiloh to worship and sacrifice to the Lord of Heaven's Armies at the Tabernacle.
4 On the days Elkanah presented his sacrifice, he would give portions of the meat to Peninnah and each of her children.
5 And though he loved Hannah, he would give her only one choice portion because the Lord had given her no children. 6 So Peninnah would taunt Hannah and make fun of her because the Lord had kept her from having children.
7 Year after year it was the same—Peninnah would taunt Hannah as they went to the Tabernacle. Each time, Hannah would be reduced to tears and would not even eat.
8 "Why are you crying, Hannah?" Elkanah would ask. "Why aren't you eating? Why be downhearted just because you have no children? You have me—isn't that better than having ten sons?"

Thousands of women could easily identify with Hannah's predicament because they've lived it. She desperately wanted to have a child, but it just wasn't happening. She and her husband had tried to conceive, but month after month the disappointment continued. It seemed she would never be a mother. Every day of her life she faced people who felt that she was a failure because she couldn't bear a child. Combine this with her already-broken heart, and you have a woman in intense pain.

Just as a shark can smell blood miles away, a hurtful person is likely to sense someone's personal pain and move in for the kill. That's what happened with the "other wife," Peninnah. Unlike Hannah, Peninnah had children, and the Bible tells us she "taunted" Hannah. For Hannah, everyday life was a challenge. Labeled a failure, unable to conceive the child she hoped for, and taunted by a jealous and difficult co-spouse, Hannah must have been completely broken.

Elkanah saw that his wife was grieving and "reduced to tears." His response was very interesting:

> *I Samuel 1:8 (NLT)*
> *8 "Why are you crying, Hannah?" Elkanah would ask. "Why aren't you eating? Why be downhearted just because you have no children?* **You have me — isn't that better than having ten sons?***" [emphasis added]*

"You have me, right? Why am I not good enough for you?" Elkanah takes Hannah's pain, instantly turns everything around, and *makes it about him.* Elkanah sees Hannah's pain and is made very uncomfortable by it. When he sees her tears it disturbs him on the inside. He can't let it go. He has to approach her about it… he has to help her understand that there is no reason to feel the way she feels. So, why do Hannah's tears make him so uncomfortable? He gives us the answer in his own words — it's because he thinks those tears mean he's a failure.

Listen to his words: "You have me — isn't that better than having ten sons?" Elkanah is saying, if you were happy with me you wouldn't be so upset. If you were satisfied with me, you wouldn't be grieving now. It's understand-able… Elkanah feels that if Hannah is happy, he is a success as a husband. If she's unhappy, he must be doing something wrong. But remember, he can't *fix this* for Hannah. He isn't in control of Hannah's ability or inabil-ity to have children. This is what makes life hard for Elkanah. His wife is hurting, and *he can't fix it.* This makes him feel like a failure, and if he's not careful, he'll make this whole situation be *about him.*

This is hugely important for you to understand. There will be many moments in your marriage where your spouse will experience deep pain that you cannot fix. This doesn't mean that you are a failure. Just as Hannah's pain *involved* Elkanah but *wasn't about* Elkanah, many times your spouse's pain will involve you but will not be about you. Unfortunately, because Elkanah fell into the trap of believing this whole thing was about him, he became angry and unsympathetic. Elkanah sent Hannah a clear message: "I can't fix this... it's not my fault! Get with the program. Be happy for Pete's sake!" Unfortunately, this message only made Hannah feel more alone.

Here's what Elkanah doesn't understand about Hannah: she knows he can't fix this. She knows he doesn't control the process of conception. She just needs him to *understand her pain and comfort her*. She needs him to realize that even when something can't be fixed, it can be made more bearable by his understanding, empathy, and tenderness. She needs to know two things. First, that Elkanah knows what she's going through, and second, that he cares. If she believes he understands how she feels and truly cares about her experience, she can cope even with a situation as difficult as this one.

Unfortunately, when this couple communicated about what they were going through, they convinced each other that they didn't care about the other's experience. It's likely that Hannah was convinced that Elkanah only cared about how this affected him and his manly pride, and Elkanah was convinced that Hannah only cared about having a child and didn't appreciate what she had in a husband like him.

Maybe this sounds familiar. Maybe sometimes when you and your spouse get into "discussions" about painful situations, perhaps you each feel like the only thing the other person cares about is themselves. If that's the case,

I'd like to give you a little tool to use to get out of the cycle of *"it's about me."* This tool will help you understand the other person, and inspire them to believe you care.

YOUR EXPERIENCE FIRST, MY EXPERIENCE NEXT...

"Your experience first, my experience next" works just like it sounds. When your spouse expresses their personal pain, you give them a chance to express it fully without interrupting or disagreeing. When they've finished expressing their experience, you help them know you understand and care by finding a way to reflect what they've said back to them. As you take the time to *talk about their experience*, you will inspire them to believe you will comfort them through their pain, and simultaneously, you give them firm footing to care about whatever pain you may be going through.

Here's an example of **what not to do**:

As a couple drives home from his mom's funeral

Husband: I can't believe she's gone... It doesn't seem real. [*His experience.*]

Wife: Yeah. I'm going to miss her so much. You know we used to sew together every Saturday. I don't know what I'll do on Saturdays anymore. I'll really miss that time together. [*Her experience.*]

Husband: I just feel numb. You just never expect to lose your mom so soon, you know? [*His experience.*]

Wife: Well, my mom died when I was fifteen. At least you had more time with your mom. I always thought you were very fortunate to still have her. I know you would have wished for more time, but I feel like you were blessed to have what you had. [*Her experience.*]

Husband: Are you serious? How can you be talking about how "fortunate" I am on the day of my mom's funeral? I'm sorry your mom died when you were a teenager, but this isn't about you... I can't believe you would say such a thing... [*His experience.*]

It's amazing how quickly a discussion between two people who "mean well" can go downhill during moments of intense pain. Let's replay this conversation with the "your experience first, my experience next" technique.

The example of **what to do**:

Husband: I can't believe she's gone... It doesn't seem real. [*His experience.*]

Wife: I imagine you must be hurting very badly right now. I'm so sorry you're having to go through this. [*She reflects his experience, next she talks about her experience.*]

It hurts for me too. I'm going to miss her so much. You know we used to sew together every Saturday. I don't know what I'll do on Saturdays anymore. I'll really miss that time together. [*Her experience.*]

Husband: I love that you and my mom enjoyed doing something together. I always loved that you shared a love of sewing in common. I bet Saturdays will be hard. We should try to do something special together. Maybe that will help. [*He reflects her experience, next he talks about his experience.*]

I just feel numb. You just never expect to lose your mom so soon, you know? [*His experience.*]

Wife: I remember feeling numb when I lost my mom. I know it's so hard to know how to respond—it's a shock to your system. I'm here for you. [*She reflects his experience, next she talks about her experience.*]

I am glad for the time you did have with your mom. Losing my mom so early on left me feeling like I missed out on so much. I'm thankful

that you and your mom had more years to
spend, even though there were not as many
as we would have liked… [*Her experience.*]

Anytime you interface with a hurting individual—even if
it's not your spouse—remember this "your experience first,
my experience next" technique. It helps the other person
to feel heard, understood, and comforted. Remember, in
this verse we are encouraged to put our spouse's needs first:

Ephesians 5:21 (NLT)
21 And further, submit to one another out of reverence
for Christ.

As we've remarked previously, the word "submit" here
means to put the other person's needs ahead of our own.
Remember though, that God doesn't ask us to ignore
or minimize our own needs or pain. He simply asks us
to put our spouse's needs and pain *first*. We are not to
ignore our own issues, but to put our spouse's issues *first*.
When your spouse goes through pain you didn't cause
and can't fix, remember that although it may involve you
it's not about you. Put their experience first, and share
your experience next. Inspire them to believe they are
heard and cared for.

REALIZATION #2: MY PRESENCE ALONE MAKES A BIG DIFFERENCE.

James Coan of the University of Virginia spearheaded a landmark scientific study about the huge impact your *presence* can make on your spouse in moments of stress or pain. He designed a study where happily married women were put in an fMRI scanner (this special piece of equipment measures activity in the brain) and told that when they saw a certain visual cue, they *might* experience a painful (but not damaging) electrical shock on their ankle. As you might imagine, this caused considerable stress and unpleasantness for the women in the experiment—especially when they saw that particular visual cue come up on the screen. They did this experiment three ways: one time with nobody else in the room, one time holding the hand of a complete stranger, and one time holding the hand of their loving husband.

After analyzing the actual brain activity recorded, and reviewing the data, Coan made the comment that "spousal hand-holding was particularly powerful." When these women were allowed to hold their husband's hand, the amount of "unpleasantness" they experienced was substantially less than when they held the hand of a stranger or were alone. The power of this finding is immense—we now know that the *actual physical response* to the threat of pain can be altered for the better, simply by the *felt presence* of the one you love. Amazing.

This is where Hannah and Elkanah were getting stuck. When Elkanah saw Hannah's tears he believed that he *had to do something*. But what? How could he change things? How could he make everything better? How could he give Hannah what she wants so that she will no longer be in pain? He can't. That's why he feels like a failure. But Hannah isn't crying because she expects Elkanah to do something. She's crying because she hurts. She lets Elkanah see her tears because the *power of his presence* has the ability to help her survive the pain she's experiencing. She doesn't expect him to *do something*. She expects him to *be there and care*.

Throughout the Bible, God gives us examples of this principle. We live in a broken world, and many times we go through circumstances that will not change. But even in the midst of those circumstances, the Bible tells us time and again that God (our primary lifeline) is with us. Take a look at just a few verses from the Bible that emphasize this point:

Genesis 39:2–3 (NLT)
*2 **The Lord was with Joseph**, so he succeeded in everything he did as he served in the home of his Egyptian master. 3 Potiphar noticed this and realized that **the Lord was with Joseph**, giving him success in everything he did.*

Genesis 39:21 (NLT)
*21 But **the Lord was with Joseph** in the prison and showed him his faithful love. And the Lord made Joseph a favorite with the prison warden.*

Exodus 3:12 (NLT)
*12 God answered, "**I will be with you**. And this is your sign that I am the one who has sent you: When you have brought the people out of Egypt, you will worship God at this very mountain."*

Joshua 1:5 (NLT)
*5 No one will be able to stand against you as long as you live. For **I will be with you** as I was with Moses. I will not fail you or abandon you.*

Isaiah 41:10 (NLT)
*10 Don't be afraid, for **I am with you**.*
Don't be discouraged, for I am your God.
I will strengthen you and help you.
I will hold you up with my victorious right hand.

Matthew 28:20 (NLT)
*20 Teach these new disciples to obey all the commands I have given you. And be sure of this: **I am with you always**, even to the end of the age."*

John 14:23 (NLT)
*23 Jesus replied, "All who love me will do what I say. My Father will love them, and **we will come and make our home with each of them**.*

Revelation 22:21 (NLT)
21 May the grace of the Lord Jesus __be with__ God's holy people.

[emphasis added in all passages]

In all of these passages, God was talking to individuals in tough circumstances. In each of their difficulties, God is reminding them that He will be with them. God didn't keep Daniel from going into the lion's den, He went along with Daniel. God didn't keep the three Hebrew children from being thrown into the fiery furnace, He went into the furnace with them. God's presence in the middle of our difficulty makes the difficulty much less dangerous. His willingness to be there for us in the middle of catastrophe allows us to face our worst fears with endurance, tenacity, and resilience.

Remember when we talked about being "God with skin on" for your spouse? This is one way that you can "imitate God" (Eph. 5:1) and be that "flesh-and-blood extension of God's love." If part of God's character is that He is always with us — even to the extent that one of His names — Emmanuel — means "God with us," then we should make this part of our own character. Our spouse should be able to depend on the fact that no matter what they go through, we will be *with* them. We may not be able to keep our spouse from experiencing deep pain, but we can walk through it with them.

Deep down, your spouse craves this. They crave the ability to know that in their darkest hours you will be by their side. Somehow, instinctively they know that this experience will hurt less if you're there with them. If you are present with them when they have to hear the bad news, when they have to say goodbye to someone they love, when they have to wait for the outcome of a difficult season of life, when they experience physical pain or emotional upheaval—you can have an incredibly positive impact on your spouse's life.

Remember, God didn't ask you to be your spouse's physician, therapist, or grief counselor. God didn't give you the responsibility of fixing every pain your spouse feels, because that would likely entail several abilities you don't have, such as resurrecting the dead and curing disease. God has only commissioned you to be there and to care. Don't underestimate the power of your presence. It's huge.

THREE KEYS TO MAXIMIZE THE POWER OF YOUR PRESENCE

Key #1: If it's beyond your ability, don't try to fix it.

My wife can vouch for the fact that God did not give me the "handyman gene." Quite frankly, I don't know what I'm doing when it comes to fixing things around the house. At a basic level, I accept that. The problem is this: despite my bad track record, every time I walk into a home improvement store I'm inspired to believe that with the right tools and materials, I could probably fix anything. I start to talk to my wife about the shower I want to re-tile, the countertops I want to replace, and the deck I want to build. My wife knows I can't do those things... but for the moment, I feel invincible. At that moment, if it's broken and in my house, you better know I can fix it.

There have been a lot of times in my marriage when I've had the very same problem. Even though I know that there are many problems Wendy and I will experience that we didn't create and can't fix, I have a strange compulsion to believe I can handle it. I think somehow I will find a way to make things be better. After all, isn't that my responsibility? Isn't it my job to find a way to fix it? No. Part of understanding how to be a success as a spouse is understanding that some problems you will experience are "above your pay grade." God will never call you to fix a problem that only He can solve.

Disclaimer: Keep in mind, we're not talking about problems you've created. If you've created difficulty for your spouse and that's the reason they're in pain, I would hope that you would try to make amends for what you've done. That's not what we're talking about here. We're talking about the pain your spouse experiences that you didn't cause and can't fix. When you face these kinds of problems, it's important *not to try to fix what you can't control and don't understand.*

Let me share a little bit of wisdom I've learned, not from my work with couples, but from hours of trying to do home improvement projects that should have taken minutes. *When you don't know how to fix something, but you try to fix it anyway, you'll usually make things worse.* This simple principle applies to marriage as well. So many times we see our spouse broken, just as Elkanah saw Hannah's tears. When we see our spouse in pain, we feel a compulsion to fix what they're going through. That's normal. That's a sign of the fact that you deeply love your spouse. But wait a minute. Can you really fix what they are going through? Are you taking on a challenge for which you don't have resources? If so, the reality is that trying to fix it will probably make it worse.

Elkanah knew Hannah was experiencing pain because she couldn't have children, and he felt compelled to try to *fix it. I'll find a way to be such a good husband to her that she doesn't even miss having kids,* he thought. *By the time I'm done stepping up my game as a husband, having kids won't even be a big blip on her radar screen.* Thoughts like these are a trap! Thinking that somehow you can fix something you can't control and don't understand is a quick way to find yourself overextended, frustrated, and experiencing new pain of your own.

Key #2: Ignoring the problem won't make it go away.

A moment ago, we talked about the fact that when you don't know how to fix something, but you try to fix it anyway, you'll usually make things worse. The truth is that many of us have discovered this fact and stopped trying to fix things some time ago. We know that much of the pain our spouse experiences can't be fixed by our own expertise, so we just *ignore* their pain. It's much easier than thinking about what they are going through and feeling like a complete failure.

I opened this chapter by talking about a couple going through the excruciating experience of losing a child to a miscarriage. Because I haven't lived it, I don't know how they feel. But what I do know is this: the husband in our story is starting to go down a very dark road. He knows he can't fix what his wife is going through, and he won't try. He doesn't realize this, but his new strategy—the "I'll just ignore it and hopefully it will go away" strategy—is perhaps even more dangerous. As he sits in his car mired in the messiness of what-if's and other unanswerable questions, he makes a choice to *ignore what he can't fix*. If he can't make it better, he'll act like it's not happening.

This may be the most important message I share with you in this entire book: *If you ignore the pain your spouse experiences, you leave them to face it alone. And loneliness defeats the purpose of marriage.*

Remember the thoughts this young mother faced? She had to cope with feelings like: *He isn't here for me and won't be. I have to face this all by myself. The only one who will be here for me is me.* Moments like this undermine the integrity of the marriage design. God designed marriage to be two people counting on one another, depending on one another, and surviving pain *with* one another.

Beware of thoughts like, *That's just the way he is; he always complains about his job. It's no big deal. He's just blowing off steam.* Or, *She always thinks other people are out to get her; she just needs to chill out. Take what she says with a grain of salt.* Or, *So she has family problems… don't we all? I don't complain about my family all the time, why can't she just suck it up? Whatever… I'm turning on the T.V.* Or, *I can't get inside his head to find out what's wrong. If he's going to sulk and mope around the house than he can just do it alone. I'm going out and finding some happy people to hang out with.*

These kinds of thoughts will take you down the road of *ignoring* your spouse's pain. If you go down this road, you will convince them that they are alone and can't count on you. I know that's not what you want.

Key #3: God has called you to face the problem with your spouse.

So if your spouse is hurting, and you can't fix it, and shouldn't ignore it, what do you do? Let's think back to James Coan's study at the University of Virginia. Remember we said that the *actual physical response* to the threat of pain can be altered for the better, simply by the *felt presence* of the one you love? I draw from these findings that the most powerful thing you can do for your spouse in these moments is to face the challenge with them. Just assuring your spouse that you will walk through this scary time with them, and that you will remain by their side will be the best thing you could choose to do.

But let's be honest... that's difficult. Sometimes even just being there — being a reliable and trustworthy presence in the middle of painful circumstances — can seem an impossible task. Fortunately, the Apostle Paul gives us some huge insight into dealing with problems that are bigger than our capabilities.

> *Hebrews 12:1b–2a (NLT)*
> *...And let us run with endurance the race God has set before us. 2 **We do this by keeping our eyes on Jesus**, the champion who initiates and perfects our faith...*
> *[emphasis added]*

If you're a marathon runner, the phrase "run with endurance" represents a familiar concept. Marathon runners know that they will have to run the majority of the race without being able to see the finish line. *To run a marathon requires both endurance and intensity — so does being there for your spouse.* When you try to *fix* your spouse's problems, the *endurance* part of the equation is missing. It's easier to try to fix the problem than patiently wait for the true resolution. On the other hand, when you try to *ignore* your spouse's problem, the *intensity* part of the equation is missing. It's easier to give up than give your best effort when your efforts don't seem to be helping.

Paul really gives us the key in the next phrase, when he reminds us to "[keep] our eyes on Jesus." Listen—when you can't fix it, and shouldn't ignore it, the best idea is to call in the Professional. As we've discussed, the do-it-yourself method of solving personal pain and difficulty doesn't work. You need to be dealing with someone who truly understands you and understands your spouse. You need someone who is no stranger to pain or grief. You need someone that can work on your behalf behind the scenes and give you comfort and peace that is better than seeing the finish line (Phil. 4:7). You need the Professional, and His name is Jesus.

> *Philippians 4:6–7 (NLT)*
> *6 Don't worry about anything; instead, pray about everything. Tell God what you need, and thank him for all he has done. 7 Then you will experience God's peace, which exceeds anything we can understand. His peace will guard your hearts and minds as you live in Christ Jesus.*

REALIZATION #3: I CAN'T DO THIS ON MY OWN.

I love to fly. I enjoy hanging out in different airports. I enjoy getting someplace fast. I even enjoy taking off and landing—the whole thing is fun for me. I especially like when the flight staff comes into the cabin and gives us the speech about all the safety equipment. There are fun parts to that drill. After all, how often do you have someone show you how to use a seatbelt? You know how the whole thing goes. They tell you where the exits are and remind you to read the terrifying emergency instruction cards they put behind all the seats. Then they break out the oxygen masks.

I've often thought that it is very interesting that when they give instructions about the use of the oxygen masks that they instruct parents to affix their masks first and *then* to place an oxygen mask on their children. Doesn't that seem a little backward? Wouldn't you expect them to recommend that you take care of a child before you see to your own needs? Well no, because if you wait to put your oxygen mask on second, you might not remain conscious long enough to put the mask on the child. You must do what's necessary to make sure that *you are healthy enough to help*. This is huge.

Often the reason that we are incapable of being there for our spouse in a moment of intense pain is that we ourselves are not emotionally healthy enough to provide that kind of support and shelter. To provide a solace to your spouse in moments of trial and difficulty, you must first find a solace. You must have an "oxygen mask" on before you try to put one on your spouse.

> *Romans 15:13 (NLT)*
> *13 I pray that God, the source of hope, will fill you completely with joy and peace because you trust in him. Then you will overflow with confident hope through the power of the Holy Spirit.*

I love what Paul says in this passage in Romans. The goal of being there for our spouse and helping them find peace in the middle of trouble and difficulty is not a matter of *providing peace for your spouse,* but a matter of *"overflowing" peace onto your spouse.* You will be able to provide the solace and shelter your spouse needs if you are actively seeking out the shelter you need in the arms of a loving God. You cannot be a flesh and blood extension of God's love to your spouse if you are not every day finding a way to explore God's love on your own.

When I was a kid, my dad used to play football in the local park with my brother and I. I guess it wasn't really football since you need more players, but we made do with what we had. One of the things I was famous for was running for the end zone to try to score a touchdown before actually catching the ball. "You have to catch it first!" my dad would holler while laughing. It seems so simple. You have to actually finish catching the ball before you can run with it. But all too often, I've made the same mistake in my relationship with Wendy. I try to comfort Wendy but I haven't even "caught" the comfort yet, and can't give what I don't have.

You need to be comforted so that you can extend comfort. Are you talking to God about your biggest problems? Are you reading His Word and putting confidence in His promises? Are you paying attention to the prayers He is answering for you? Just as we need air to breathe, we need God's comfort in our lives. Each of us needs to personally experience God's incredible love so that we can share it.

In summary, don't try to fix what you don't understand and can't control, you'll probably make it worse. But, on the other hand, don't ignore the problem and just hope it will eventually go away. Just be ready and willing to stand shoulder to shoulder with your spouse and face the challenges and pain together. Don't quit doing what you know to do just because you're tired of not seeing the outcome you're looking for. You must keep up the intensity even when the finish line is not yet in sight. Don't quit. Your spouse needs you. Remember to run with patience. Call in the professional. Ask God for the help you need, and receive his comfort—you need it as much as your spouse does.

Dear God,
It's good to know that You understand the pain we face in this relationship. No matter how tough the circumstance, I know that You can help us through. Please keep me from making something worse by thinking I can fix a problem I don't understand. Remind me not to quit when I feel like I'm failing or when the problem seems too big to face. Give me the strength I need to comfort my spouse by facing these challenges with them. I know You will never let us down. We need Your strength now. I trust You.

Chapter 5

YOUR SPOUSE NEEDS YOUR SUPPORT

For years, my wife and I lived in the Oklahoma City area. Early on, we learned that college football was a very important part of the local culture. Just to the south of Oklahoma City is the city of Norman, home to the University of Oklahoma, lovingly referred to as OU. Stillwater, Oklahoma is about an hour northeast of Oklahoma City, and is home to Oklahoma State University. Both of these schools have enormous fan bases in the OKC metro. Just about everyone I met rooted for one of these two teams—even people who had never set foot on either campus.

Most of the time I lived in Oklahoma, I worked alongside OU fans. Sometimes OU played well, other times they tripped over their shoes. (Sorry OU fans; it's true.) But it seemed that no matter how the game ended, my friends remained fans. OU could lose badly—they could make terrible mistakes that cost them the game—but my friends still wore the "crimson and cream" team colors and walked around saying stuff like, "We'll get 'em next year."

Often I would have individuals ask me which team I rooted for. "Whichever team is winning," I'd say with a smile. The truth is that I don't really follow college sports, and so it was my way of saying that I don't have any particular *loyalty* for either team. My friends did. That's why they didn't quit being fans just because their team lost. That's why they weren't ashamed to continue supporting their athletes even after a depressing defeat.

My friends had made a decision before the game was ever played. They were OU fans and they always would be. Their loyalty didn't hinge on the outcome of a specific game or season. They knew before the opening coin toss that they would either celebrate the victory of the win, or overcome the difficulty of the loss, and they would emerge — as they started — completely committed to the team they support.

I cannot begin to tell you how my heart longs to see the same kind of loyalty in the couples I serve. I see it sometimes, but it's rare. Often couples come into my office to "determine what's possible" or "see if we might be able to make this work." Instead of assuming the marriage can and will work with the right help, some couples I work with have already assumed it probably won't work and they are giving me a "shot" at helping them as a last resort. Don't get me wrong — I'm grateful for the opportunity to help — but where's the loyalty? How is it that we can watch a football game and think "we'll get 'em next time," but we can't look at our marriages with the same kind of resilient hope?

In most of our relationships, we anticipate a balance between success and failure. We know our friends will mess up sometimes, but we also see their redeeming qualities. Sometimes in marriage, though, we begin to take the redeeming qualities for granted. We can minimize the ways in which our spouse is successful, and accidentally spend our time focusing on the areas in which we believe they fail. When this happens, we often leave our spouse to believe that they will never be good enough, and that no matter how hard they try, they will always be reaching for an impossible goal.

NOT A FAN.

During a particularly busy day at the hospital, Clint found himself behind schedule by about twenty minutes. *Guess I'll have to make that up somewhere,* he thought. *There goes lunch.* Clint was a highly respected surgeon, but time and tide wait for no man. He had to get moving. As he passed the nurse's station, one of the female nurses stopped him for a moment. "Clint, Miss Davis in Room 820 looks so much better since the procedure. We were really worried about having to put her back on dialysis, and according to her physician, it looks like she's not even going to need it. I wish you did all the procedures for the patients on this floor, I'll tell you that." Clint demurred but appreciated the complement. After all, he had worked hard to become a success in his field. It felt nice to have his efforts recognized.

The hospital was undergoing a renovation that included the addition of a new wing, and the president of the hospital was counting on Clint to help him publicize the need for outside financial contributions. (As if Clint had nothing else on his plate.) As Clint flew down the hallway he ran into the hospital president.

"Lunch tomorrow, Clint?"

"Sure, you bet!" Clint replied.

"Thanks, buddy. We couldn't do this without you."

Another pat on the back—Clint was two for two. It felt good to know that the hospital had confidence in him.

Clint headed to his private office to do some consultations before heading home.

"I don't know how you do it," his secretary said, as he managed to make it in the door just in time. "One way or another you always seem to come through. Your first consult is in Room 3."

By the end of Clint's day he was completely exhausted. Maybe he was taking on too much, but it sure felt good to have so many people believe in him. The nurses, his administrative staff, the hospital staff—everybody seemed to trust that he was capable, hard working, and talented.

As he entered the front door of his home, he knew his day was about to take a significant shift. While everyone in his professional life seemed to think he could do no wrong, his wife seemed to think he could do nothing right. She called out to him as he entered the house.

"Geez, Clint, why didn't you call? I swear that's the fourth time you've been late in the last two weeks. This is ridiculous. You can perform major surgery, but you can't pick up a phone and place a two-minute call? What's the excuse this time?"

"No excuse. I was busy, okay?" Clint replied curtly.

"By the way," she added, "The car dealership called. You didn't show up for your appointment to get your oil changed. What's up with that?"

"I had to make up for twenty minutes somewhere today," Clint replied. "The car will just have to wait. It's not the end of the world, you know."

Then Clint did what he usually does. He went to his "TV room" and zoned. For the rest of the evening, Clint did something that made no sense to his wife. He acted like she wasn't even there. In the early years of their marriage they used to have fights about these kinds of discussions. Clint would angrily express how hurt he was that she always paid attention to his flaws and not his good points, and Clint's wife would emphasize how difficult it was to live with those flaws. They never came to any understanding, and so eventually they settled into this new routine. The fights were a thing of the past for the most part. Now, it was quiet most of the time… a little too quiet.

Clint and his wife are not alone in going through this kind of difficulty. In the Bible, King David and his wife Michal had similar problems. The story is a very long one, but the short version goes something like this.

Before David became King, he worked for his predecessor, King Saul. Saul had a daughter named Michal. The Bible tells us that Michal had "fallen in love" with David.

> *1 Samuel 18:20a (NLT)*
> *20 In the meantime, Saul's daughter Michal had fallen in love with David…*

And David must have loved her too… he was willing to take on an almost-impossible military task in order to win the privilege of marrying her. To the female readers of this book, I challenge you to imagine: how would you feel if a guy loved you enough to put his life on the line in the hopes that he might somehow earn the privilege to ask for your hand in marriage? Make no mistake about it, Michal loved David, and David loved Michal.

> *1 Samuel 18:28–29 (NLT)*
> *28 When Saul realized that the Lord was with David and **<u>how much his daughter Michal loved him</u>**, 29 Saul*

became even more afraid of him, and he remained David's enemy for the rest of his life. [emphasis added]

After the wedding, Michal still loved David fiercely. Even her dad — the current king of Israel — took notice. Saul didn't turn out to be a very kind father-in-law. He was paranoid because deep down he knew David was eventually going to get his job, so he became David's personal enemy from that time on. Amazingly, at one point, Saul actually sent soldiers to David's house to kill him while his daughter was there. Michal's love for David was so strong that she found a way to smuggle him out of the house before her father had a chance to kill him.

> *1 Samuel 19:11–12 (NLT)*
> *11 Then Saul sent troops to watch David's house. They were told to kill David when he came out the next morning. But Michal, David's wife, warned him, "If you don't escape tonight, you will be dead by morning." 12 So she helped him climb out through a window, and he fled and escaped.*

I'm giving you the details of this story so that you will realize that David and Michal had a very special relationship. But sometime later they would hit a major marital snag and it would center on this issue of support. It's the story of a meltdown. To David and anyone who seriously followed God in those days, the Ark of the Covenant was of incredible importance. This gold-encrusted wooden box symbolized God's presence, and often God would make his presence known through this object.

Before David came to power, the Ark had been stolen by the enemies of God's people. God's enemies didn't know what to do with it, so they eventually returned it. However, the Ark of the Covenant stayed in a "neutral zone" for some time until David became king. David wanted to retrieve the Ark, and made an attempt, but it ended in failure, and David temporarily gave up.

Eventually, David and God were on the same page, and David was ready to try again to restore the Ark to its rightful home where God's people worshiped — the tabernacle. When David set out to recover the Ark, the Bible tells us that he got pretty excited about the whole thing, and started dancing for the Lord "with all his might."

> *2 Samuel 6:14–15 (NLT)*
> *14 And David danced before the Lord with all his might, wearing a priestly garment. 15 So David and all the people of Israel brought up the Ark of the Lord with shouts of joy and the blowing of rams' horns.*

David was wearing a priestly garment that probably left something to be desired in terms of modesty. Michal — David's wife — saw the dance from the window of the palace and wasn't happy.

> *2 Samuel 6:20 (NLT)*
> *20 When David returned home to bless his own family, Michal, the daughter of Saul, came out to meet him. She said in disgust, "How distinguished the king of Israel looked*

today, shamelessly exposing himself to the servant girls like any vulgar person might do!"

David was floored. Where was this coming from? Didn't she know that this was one of the biggest moments of his life? Didn't she know that bringing the Ark of the covenant back to the tabernacle would be one of his most important achievements? How could she be mad at him for dancing for God? He wasn't trying to do anything wrong… he was trying to show God—and the people of Israel—how wonderful and important this moment was. Michal was probably legitimately offended by her husband's lack of modesty in this instance, but David wouldn't be able to hear her concern—all he heard was her complete lack of support for him.

2 Samuel 6:21–22 (NLT)
21 David retorted to Michal, "I was dancing before the Lord, who chose me above your father and all his family! He appointed me as the leader of Israel, the people of the Lord, so I celebrate before the Lord. 22 Yes, and I am willing to look even more foolish than this, even to be humiliated in my own eyes! But those servant girls you mentioned will indeed think I am distinguished!"

What was David saying to his wife? "You don't get me. You don't look for the good in me anymore… you look for the bad in me. God has given me a responsibility, and you act like it's no big deal. Well… you think today was undignified? You haven't seen anything yet. You may be worried about what those servant girls think of me, but

I'll tell you something… at least they think well of me. That's more than I can say for you."

> *2 Samuel 6:23 (NLT)*
> *23 So Michal, the daughter of Saul, remained childless throughout her entire life.*

I believe that the above verse means that on this day David and Michal's marriage came to a screeching halt. I believe at this point they were married in name only. Like Clint and his wife, David and Michal started living separate lives because the support system just wasn't there anymore. Clint believed that everyone in his life saw good in him except for his wife. Similarly, David felt like the servant girls in his kingdom viewed him with greater respect and honor than his own wife.

Clint's wife and Michal both had legitimate reasons to be upset. Perhaps Clint should have called to let his wife know he would be late, and it likely hurt Michal's feelings to see David being immodest in the presence of other women — even for a good reason. Perhaps in your marriage, you recognize an area where your spouse is failing, and it may be very important to you. Just remember, there's a monumental difference between *talking to your spouse about a failure*, and *treating your spouse like a failure*. Clint and David had to wrestle with the realization that their spouses didn't see "the best in them" anymore. Do you see the best in your spouse? Are you a fan?

In the arena of life, your spouse will eventually look back at their "corner" to see who believes in them. One of three things will happen. Either you will be the person who supports them, someone else will, or they will find themselves completely on their own. For my part, I don't want Wendy to ever feel like she has no one in her corner, and I certainly don't want someone else to take my place supporting her—that's my job. I want her to always know that when she needs someone to "have her back" that she can count on me. I want her to know that I believe in her and that even if she fails I will still support her.

In this short chapter, I want to give you three keys to being a fan of your spouse. This doesn't mean that you don't see areas in which they need to improve, it simply means that you want to show your spouse that you don't see them as a failure, and that you have the ability to believe the best about them.

THREE KEYS TO BEING YOUR SPOUSE'S #1 FAN

Key #1: Show Up

I know this sounds elementary, but it can't be overstated: *You can't be a support system if you're not present.* In David and Michal's relationship, this was part of the crisis. It's clear from the Scripture that women went along with the group that brought back the Ark, and that they participated in the celebration. Michal didn't go. We don't know exactly why, and there may have been a good reason, but the Scriptures lead us to believe that she didn't go because *she didn't want to.*

David was a success in many areas of his life, and it's highly possible that Michal stopped fully appreciating these victories simply because she quit being there to see them. Similarly, Clint's wife didn't frequent the hospital. There didn't seem to be any good reason to do so. But one day she decided to surprise him by showing up unexpectedly at the hospital to take him out to lunch. She had to wait a while for him to get out of surgery, and as she waited, she spoke with several members of the hospital staff. She was amazed at all the incredible things they had to say about her husband. Apparently, he was some kind of medical genius. She didn't know that. How could she? She was never there. She never took the time to visit his world.

The hospital gave certain privileges to doctors, and one of the privileges Clint received was a small office in the hospital complex. Clint's wife stepped inside his office to think. As she considered what she had heard and seen at the hospital she noticed several plaques and trophies on his small bookshelf.

He won these, she thought. *Why didn't he bring these home?* Then it dawned on her. *At work, he's a success; at home he feels like a failure. No wonder I'm not part of his world anymore; I've stopped trying to be part of it.*

Lest anyone think that I am picking on Clint's wife, let me just say that I think Clint has behaved just as hurtfully by holding her at arm's length. Clint's wife didn't have a mean or hurtful bone in her body. She truly wanted to see her marriage improve, and the marriage problems she and Clint experienced were not all her fault. But her realization was crucial. Clint truly did need to know that she wanted to be part of his world. He needed her to care about the areas in which he was a success before he was ready to be confronted with the areas in which he fails.

Even if you're not married to a medical genius, let me assure you that your spouse is passionate about *something*, and that passion is very important to them. Nothing will energize your spouse like knowing that when they take on life's challenges you will be present to support and cheer them on.

For the last few years, my oldest daughter has played team sports in the summer. It started with tee-ball, and now she is playing softball. I've noticed that at these games, the young athletes on the field often cast a glance to the bleachers scanning faces and looking for their parents in the crowd. Nobody has to teach these kids to do this. They instinctively care about whether or not their parents have "shown up" to cheer them on. When we were kids we acted the same way. We may have grown up, but we never grew out of the need to be believed in.

Jesus teaches us a very important principle about "showing up" in this verse.

Matthew 6:21 (NLT)
*21 Wherever your treasure is, there the desires of your heart
will also be.*

What Jesus teaches us here is a very simple principle
(that we'll visit again in Chapter 8): *your heart will always
follow your investment.* When you invest your heart and
soul in something, you can anticipate that you will care
deeply about it. This teaches us that if you make it a point
to show up and invest in something that your spouse is
passionate about, you will actually *begin to care about* your
spouse's goals. If you never show up and don't invest in
what drives your spouse, you will *automatically* get to a
point where you don't care about their passions.

This is an area where you could see substantial improvement in your relationship very quickly. Think about
making a choice to invest in something your spouse deeply
cares about. What can you do to show them that you
want to see them succeed in an area that represents their
biggest challenge? Start making investments in their
dreams and watch your relationship grow. You might be
surprised to find out how much your spouse will come
to depend on you if you make it a point to *show up* and
invest in their success.

Key #2: Make Some [Positive] Noise

Recently I was at a locally owned restaurant waiting for
the food we had ordered, when I overheard a discussion
in the kitchen.

"I hate that stupid comment box," one employee said. "We can have 999 customers who are completely satisfied and thrilled with our service, and the one customer who gets their feathers ruffled is the only person who manages to fill out a blasted card and stick it in the box."

I couldn't help but chuckle at the honesty of the employee's statement. That does seem to be the way things go. It seems like we're more likely to go out of our way to identify a problem than to talk about a recognized strength.

For example: I like my steaks medium rare. But my track record lately hasn't been very good at getting steaks that are cooked that way. The last couple of times I ordered steak at a restaurant, they brought me a piece of meat that was so rare, it might have still been alive. It's interesting that I have absolutely no issue calling the waiter over to my table and insisting that they put the steak on the grill longer, and yet, I can't remember the last time I called my waiter over to express my gratitude for a steak that was properly prepared.

The title of this section is "make some [positive] noise." This is what fans do. They make noise to encourage the team they support and to inspire them to do their very best. Sadly, sometimes I make noise in my relationship with Wendy, but it's the wrong kind of noise. Instead of voicing my support and cheering her on, I use my words to tell her where she is failing and what she should be doing better. Just as Wendy needs my words of encouragement, your spouse needs to *hear* you express your belief in them.

I am beginning to recognize that I often take "great" for granted. I have a great wife and great kids. I serve a great God and have a great job. I experience great opportunities and am surrounded by great influences. All of these incredible advantages are gifts — gifts from God to me — and yet I do not often express my gratitude for them. I am much more likely to talk about something that makes me mad or unhappy than to talk about all the great things God has given me.

I have given Wendy the whole "we need to talk" routine before to open up the dialogue about something that I think she's doing wrong. Frankly, I can't remember the last time I told Wendy "we need to talk" so that I can tell her all of the things she is doing well. I want to live reminded of the fact that Wendy needs me to "make some noise" that inspires her to believe she can take on life's challenges and succeed. She needs me to be that annoying fan that has the noisemakers, the megaphone and the air horn — anything that I can use to let her know that she's number one as far as I'm concerned.

Clint's wife actually did think that she was married to a pretty cool guy. Sure, she sometimes got upset with him, but she saw that he had many good points. When she spent time in her women's Bible study she often remarked to the other ladies in the group how wonderful Clint was with their kids.

"He's a good dad," she would say, "and he's so smart... you know he graduated at the top of his class in medical school..."

Clint's wife actually admired her husband in many ways. She just didn't tell *him* about it. When she "made noise" in the relationship it was to let him know where he was messing up, not to thank him for what he was doing well.

As she walked through the hallways of the hospital she thought, *Everyone here cheers him on to succeed. No wonder he seems so driven to accomplish big things here.* It dawned on her that while she loved her husband, she had quit cheering him on some time ago. Her new method for motivating him had been to express her frustration and hope he would get a clue. She now realized that all the frustration she had been venting had inspired him to conclude that she didn't believe in him anymore.

But she did believe in him. And unless I miss my guess, you believe in your spouse, too. Sure, you see their faults—that's part of being with someone all the time. But you also see their good points. It's so important that you *use your words to express* the fact that you appreciate your spouse's strengths and that you believe in them. Remember, your spouse doesn't know what you're thinking. They only know what you're saying.

Proverbs 18:21a (NLT)
21 The tongue can bring death or life...

What you have to say is huge. Your words will either build up, or they will tear down. What kind of noise are you making in your relationship? Are you inspiring your spouse to believe they can take on the biggest challenges of their life, or are you giving them reason to believe they will probably fail and that their mistakes are more important than their successes? Your spouse needs you. They need your support. If the noise in your relationship has been hurtful so far, take this moment to commit to a turnaround. Break out the megaphones and pom-poms — you can do this!

Key #3: Don't Give Up

Years ago, before I went into the ministry, I remember watching bits and pieces of a college football game on TV with co-workers. The game was interesting to me because torrential rain was pouring down on the field. I didn't know how the athletes could even see anything. The other interesting part was that the game — now in the fourth quarter — might as well be over. One team was absolutely crushing the other. I'll never forget watching the cameras pan to the bleachers where the fans of the losing team sat.

There they were… drenched and disappointed… *but not leaving.* I kept thinking to myself, *The game's basically over… why don't they just go find someplace warm and dry?*

I didn't understand what it meant to truly be a fan. If you really believe in your team and you truly support them, you don't just get up and walk away because of a little rain or because the scoreboard tells a depressing story. *You stay with the team you support.*

Wendy and I have not always enjoyed the great marriage we have today. In the early years of our relationship we truly struggled just to get along. In the middle of dealing with our issues as a couple, I would often get frustrated and desperate and suggest that she should just leave me. I would say things like, "Then why don't you just divorce me?" or "If you don't like living with me, you know what you can do about it." Later as our struggles became more intense, I started to threaten to leave. I would say things like, "I don't deserve to have to deal with this. I should just get out now while I have the chance."

I'm not at all proud of my behavior in those days. Deep down I knew that my actions and words were not only hurting Wendy, they were disappointing God. After all, when we were married, I promised God that I would stay with Wendy for better or worse. I wasn't living up to my end of the bargain. But at the time, *being her fan* wasn't high on my priority list, and walking away felt like the most sensible thing to do.

One day after we had received some counseling and were doing much better we suffered a minor setback. We started arguing about something small and insignificant, and, as was our pattern, it became a big fight.

"Why don't you just leave then?" I remember saying.

I'll never forget my wife's response. As mad as she was, she responded, "Because you're stuck with me! Remember? The two of us, together... that's the way this thing works. You're staying with me and I'm staying with you, so enough of this leaving talk. If we're going to fight, then let's fight, but you're not going anywhere and I'm not either. We're a couple, and that's that."

Something clicked for me when she said those words. My wife had just said that she wasn't going to leave me no matter what. She had just indicated that whether we were having a good time together, or struggling, she would be right there by my side. It may not sound romantic that my wife said I was "stuck with her," but it may have been one of the most beautiful things she has ever said to me. She was letting me know that no matter what we go through as a couple she would be there going through it with me. She didn't want me to talk about leaving anymore because that's not even up for discussion if you're a true fan. True fans don't talk about leaving. If you have a true fan, you're stuck with them. Be thankful for that.

Have you made a decision to "stick with" your spouse no matter what? Even if you go through stress and times of difficulty are you willing to remain loyal? Your spouse desperately needs to know that you will be there to support them no matter what they go through. Don't forget to show up and invest in what they are passionate about. Make some positive noise to remind them that you see the best in them, and then make a commitment not to quit. Don't walk away. Your spouse needs you.

Dear God,
Help me as I try to be my spouse's biggest fan. Sometimes it's hard to see the best in an imperfect person, but I know You do that for me, and I want to do the same for my spouse. Help me to know how to invest in the things that my spouse truly cares about. Help me to say things that would encourage them to believe that I support their success. I pray You would allow me to stick with my commitment to be there for my spouse, even when I feel like walking away. You've never quit being there for me. Help me to always be there for my spouse.

Chapter 6

YOUR SPOUSE NEEDS
YOUR ACCEPTANCE

The sound of the alarm clock roused Cynthia from warm, comfortable sleep for the fifth time. She had a bad habit of hitting the snooze several times and waking up "gradually."

I hate mornings, she thought.

As she stumbled out of bed she heard a clanking sound in the kitchen. *Fantastic,* she thought sarcastically, *Keith's still here.*

Cynthia's husband Keith always made a point to rise at 5:30 a.m. After eating a healthy breakfast, Keith would get on the treadmill and exercise while watching the morning news. Then, while sipping his morning coffee, Keith would draw out a task list for the day. *A morning routine like that would kill me,* Cynthia thought.

Years ago when they were dating, Keith saw Cynthia's morning habits as "cute" and "quirky." He told his friends how cool it was that she was a "laid back" person. Now Cynthia's "laid back" nature was really starting to grate on his nerves.

"Good morning, sleepyhead," Keith said to Cynthia as she walked into the kitchen.

To an uninformed bystander, this may sound like an innocuous morning greeting, but Cynthia and Keith knew the truth. His comment was an insult. It was the first of many "jabs" Cynthia would receive from Keith during the day.

Cynthia had been at work for a couple of hours before she received a phone call from the automotive shop that had been working on her car for two weeks. "Cynthia, I'm sorry to tell you this, but there's been another time delay and it looks like your car will have to stay in the shop for another couple of days. Also, our original estimate has unfortunately been exceeded again. We would have called you to get your approval first, but we know you're a busy lady, so we went ahead with the work. It looks like you're going to owe us about $400 more than we originally discussed. That won't be a huge deal, will it?"

Cynthia didn't know how to answer. She hated dealing with this kind of problem. She told the mechanic she would call back and quickly dialed her husband. "Keith, I don't know what to do with these car people," she said, "I think they're taking advantage of me. All I want is to get my car back and have it run. Can you call them and straighten them out?"

Keith answered, "Cynthia, you've got to start handling things like this yourself. I know you hate confrontation, but you just need to get over it. I'm busy. Take care of it yourself. *Love you.*"

That evening, Keith and Cynthia attended a retirement party for one of Keith's co-workers. Cynthia was uncomfortable going to events like this. Trying to mingle and carry on conversations with complete strangers was intimidating and she didn't like it. She was not an outgoing person, although she wished she could be. One by one, Keith introduced her to his co-workers and friends. Cynthia smiled and nodded as Keith talked shop and cracked inside jokes. *I so don't belong here...* Cynthia thought. She knew she was being quiet and reserved, but that was *who she was.* She tried to be pleasant and gracious — that was the best she could do.

In the car on the way home Keith was silent and withdrawn.

Cynthia let out a sigh. "What did I do?" she asked with resignation.

"It's what you didn't do," Keith replied. "You were the only woman at that party tonight who wasn't full of conversation and energy. You were a stick in the mud. Why can't you step out of your shell for just one night and show the world some verve and excitement? Why do you have to be such an introvert?"

Realizing that he was insulting his wife, Keith tried to put a positive spin on his critical words. "I know that deep down inside you're an exciting, vibrant person… I just want my friends and co-workers to meet the real you."

The conversation ended as quietly as it started. Cynthia did not reply. She had learned that replying didn't help. She just let her husband vent about what he didn't like about her.

Later that evening, Keith and Cynthia watched a movie together on the couch. The unpleasantness of the evening started to dissipate as they enjoyed the humorous and romantic movie. Keith embraced Cynthia and kissed her tenderly.

He wants to make love to me, Cynthia thought. *It's been kind of a rough day, but I do want to meet his needs, and at the moment I feel kind of close to him. He loves having sex with me… at least that's one thing he won't critique.*

"I'll meet you in the bedroom in five minutes," she said to Keith.

Five minutes was what she needed. She needed to collect herself. She'd lived though a difficult day. At every turn she felt her husband's disapproval of her. Now the evening seemed to be heading in a better direction. She needed some time to de-stress and feel normal again. She needed to take a moment or two to reorient her thinking, and find a way to relax into an evening of intimacy with her husband. As she washed off her makeup and slipped into some comfortable pajamas, she thought, *At least it's nice to end the day on a good note.*

When Keith entered the room, she read the look of extreme disappointment on his face.

"Is this what you needed five minutes for?" he asked, pointing to her. "I thought when you said you needed five minutes that you were going to slip into something sexy and seductive like that outfit I bought you last Valentine's Day. You know that outfit turns me on. Why would you ask me for five minutes to put on your pajamas? It's kind of disappointing, you know?"

Pause the tape. At this point Cynthia is crushed. How could she not be? All day she has not been good enough for her husband. She doesn't wake up early enough, she's not assertive enough, she's not social enough, and now she's not sexy enough. This is about all one person can take. Cynthia feels trapped. How can she face each day of the rest of her life knowing that her husband will view her as a disappointment?

She feels as though Keith wants her to be a *different woman.* She knows that no matter how much she grows as a person, and no matter how much she works to achieve compromise with Keith, she will still be Cynthia. Ultimately, she will still be who she is. If, in the end, she is not good enough for him, she will live her life feeling like a failure. This is an overwhelming thought to her.

When Cynthia and Keith came to see me for marriage coaching, they were both extremely frustrated. Keith didn't understand why his wife felt persecuted by him, and Cynthia was amazed that Keith could not see how badly he was hurting her. Repeatedly, Cynthia said, "*I'll never be good enough for him.*" And she meant it. She truly believed that Keith would always see her as a substandard human being. This was a debilitating reality for her, and the marriage was paying a severe price for the resulting disconnection.

What Cynthia is really struggling with is the need to be *accepted*. She needs her husband to like who she is as a person despite her shortcomings and personal failings. Cynthia would love for Keith to be a source of strength for her when she encounters areas in which she struggles or experiences difficulties. Unfortunately, when Keith sees these personal failings in Cynthia, he harshly exposes, criticizes and rejects them. As a result, Cynthia feels exposed, criticized, and rejected. In this state, Cynthia feels wounded and abandoned by the person that should be protecting her.

THE PROBLEM OF IMPERFECTION

Throughout the New Testament Gospels (Matthew, Mark, Luke and John) there is this tremendous ongoing tension between Jesus and a group of individuals referred to as the Pharisees. The Pharisees opposed Jesus, but not because they were anti-religion, or anti-God. As a matter of fact, the Pharisees spent their lives "cornering the market" on religion. They made it their personal mission to epitomize the kind of people God approved of. Even though they were imperfect, they began to feel empowered by whatever level of perfection they thought they had achieved. This ended up being their downfall. "Perfection" was their goal, and as a result, they became unwilling to recognize imperfection in themselves, and uncomfortable with imperfection in others.

This kept the Pharisees from being able to accept other people who did not also appear to be perfect. Jesus called them out about this when he told the story of two men going to the temple to pray.

> *Luke 18:10–14 (NLT)*
> *10 "Two men went to the Temple to pray. One was a Pharisee, and the other was a despised tax collector. 11 The Pharisee stood by himself and prayed this prayer: 'I thank you, God, that I am not a sinner like everyone else. For I don't cheat, I don't sin, and I don't commit adultery. I'm certainly not like that tax collector! 12 I fast twice a week, and I give you a tenth of my income.'*
> *13 "But the tax collector stood at a distance and dared not even lift his eyes to heaven as he prayed. Instead, he beat his chest in sorrow, saying, 'O God, be merciful to me, for I am a sinner.' 14 I tell you, this sinner, not the Pharisee, returned home justified before God. For those who exalt themselves will be humbled, and those who humble themselves will be exalted."*

In this story, not only does the Pharisee not accept the tax collector, he uses the publican's sin as leverage to make himself feel better. What does the Pharisee get out of praying a prayer like this? He certainly doesn't get the benefit of some tremendous connection to God, because in this passage Jesus — who is God — is explaining the uselessness of such a prayer. No, I think the main function of this Pharisee's prayer was to make himself feel better. The more imperfection he could spot in another person, the less imperfect he felt personally.

The Pharisee used his prayer life to point out other people's faults and feel better about himself. In marriage, though, we more often use our critical tongue to insult our spouse directly, saying things like:

"Well, I just don't think you're doing a very good job disciplining our children. Look how they behave."

"I think you could find better ways to spend your time, don't you?"

"If I can volunteer at church, why can't you? You should get off your duff and do something."

"When will you ever start picking up after yourself around here? I swear you're worse than the children sometimes."

"Why do you always have to be so quiet? Would it kill you to open up and say something sometime?"

In the story of Keith and Cynthia, we talked about how Keith mentioned all the areas in which he felt she needed to improve. He viewed her as deficient in these areas, just as the Pharisee viewed the tax collector as being a deficient person. In order for Keith to feel "good" about himself, he needed to point out the "bad" in Cynthia, and he did so on a regular basis.

Keith didn't realize he was doing this, just as the Pharisee might also not have realized that he was stuck in the "I'm better than you" mindset. A Pharisee like the one in Jesus' story would have "worshipped" at the temple daily, praying similar prayers. While this story was one of many parables Jesus used, it could have easily been a true story. Many Pharisees at that time were guilty of praying similar prayers. Day after day these men made themselves feel better by comparing their "dirty laundry" to other people's "dirty laundry." What they did not realize is that ultimately they were fooling themselves.

> *Matthew 23:25–26 (NLT)*
> *25 "What sorrow awaits you teachers of religious law and you Pharisees. Hypocrites! For you are so careful to clean the outside of the cup and the dish, but inside you are filthy—full of greed and self-indulgence! 26 You blind Pharisee! First wash the inside of the cup and the dish, and then the outside will become clean, too."*

In this passage, Jesus calls the Pharisees blind. This statement is particularly interesting since this entire book is about how to be able to see your marriage clearly again.

So why did Jesus say they were blind? How did they lose that all important "vision" we talked about in Chapter 1? By *always looking outside* and *never looking inside*. There was an ugly truth inside the lives of each of these pious Pharisees that none of them cared to embrace. That truth was that they were imperfect. It was very difficult for them to accept this because they had come to believe that achieving some level of perfection was the way to attain God's approval.

Like many of us, the Pharisees had come to a place in their lives where projecting a near-perfect image was the only way to make sense of the world. If they had to examine and embrace their own imperfection, their view of the world fell apart. This is a dangerous emotional place to be. The fact that the Pharisees were instrumental in the betrayal and prosecution of Jesus Christ stemmed from the fact that facing the reality Jesus brought was too painful for them. They could not be exposed for what they were. They would rather kill someone than look inside.

Think for a moment about the huge contrast between people who tried hard to portray themselves as perfect — the Pharisees — and someone who really was perfect — Jesus Christ. The Pharisees worked hard to distance themselves from "sinners," and Jesus worked hard to engage sinners. This truth is evident from a simple exchange we find in the book of Mark.

> *Mark 2:16 (NLT)*
> *16 But when the teachers of religious law who were Pharisees saw him eating with tax collectors and other sinners,*

they asked his disciples, "Why does he eat with such scum?"

In this passage, look at how the Pharisees suggest Jesus shouldn't even be eating with the individuals they referred to as "scum." Jesus, unlike the Pharisees, was willing to get close to imperfect people… to get to know them and love them. It should have been no surprise that Jesus spent His time showing love to imperfect people, as His ministry culminated in the ultimate expression of love for broken individuals—His death on the cross.

Jesus had no problem sitting at a well and talking with a woman who had been married five times and was now sleeping with a man who was not her husband. He had no problem trying to explain the basic Gospel message to a man who had studied prophetic Scriptures his whole life and just didn't "get it." He had no problem breaking bread with individuals who were liars, cheaters, and adulterers. The bottom line: *Jesus loved imperfect people.* It's time for a reality check. How do we feel about our own imperfection, and the imperfection of others?

"Imperfect" Is To Be Expected

In the deepest place of each of our hearts, we know that we are not perfect. When we're honest with ourselves, we know that there are lots of areas in our lives in which we need to repent, grow, or improve. But this is a hard reality to cope with, because none of us like to face our own failures. Life would be so much more pleasant for all of us if we could just be perfect and quit causing pain for ourselves and others. Someday in heaven we will experience that kind of life. For now, failure is part of the equation.

> *Romans 5:12 (NLT)*
> *12 When Adam sinned, sin entered the world. Adam's sin brought death, so death spread to everyone, for everyone sinned.*

According to the Bible, Adam's sin created a new paradigm in which all human beings experience failure. But even the apostle Paul was transparent enough to share in Romans that this reality was very difficult for him. He talked about an internal war between the part of him that wanted to be perfect, and the part of him that kept failing.

> *Romans 7:15a,18b-20 (NLT)*
> *15 I don't really understand myself, for I want to do what is right, but I don't do it. Instead, I do what I hate...*
> *...I want to do what is right, but I can't. 19 I want to do what is good, but I don't. I don't want to do what is wrong, but I do it anyway. 20 But if I do what I don't want to do, I am not really the one doing wrong; it is sin living in me that does it.*

Maybe you can relate to Paul. Perhaps, like Paul, you wish you could do everything right, but you consistently find yourself struggling and doing the wrong thing. If so, be encouraged! You're in good company. If the author of the majority of the books in the New Testament realized his frustration with his own unmet desire to always do the right thing, there's nothing wrong with your feeling the same inner unrest.

Keith, in our earlier story, was really struggling with this reality. He knew there were imperfect parts of himself, but he worked diligently to hide and overcome those parts. He did not like to approach the part of himself that was imperfect, because that part of him felt like a dismal failure. He was unable to admit, like Paul, that he wanted to do good but wasn't doing it. His mind constantly struggled with the question, "How can I be a good person and not be doing all the right things?" As a result, the only way he could feel like the world made sense was to lie to himself and try to believe that he was doing things "right."

When Cynthia did something "wrong," it angered Keith, but he didn't know why. He didn't care to realize that Cynthia's imperfection made him uncomfortable because the very concept of imperfection was not something he was ready to deal with. Keith desperately wanted to avoid dealing with his own personal failure, and seeing those areas where Cynthia failed hit a little too close to home. Just as he had "schooled" himself on how to do things "correctly," he made it his mission in life to "school" Cynthia and help her achieve the kind of success that would be validating not only for her, but also — and most importantly — for him.

How To Deal With Imperfection:
Finding a New Standard of Measurement

Shortly after marrying Wendy, I decided I wanted to train to become a car mechanic. I went to a nationally-known automotive school and studied very hard. After I graduated, I was offered a job as a mechanic at a large car dealership in the Midwest. When I started there, they provided me with a "starter" tool set. I had a bit of a problem right away, though, because the majority of the tools they provided corresponded to the "standard" or "SAE" unit of measure, and most of the automobiles I worked on had "metric" fittings. Because my tools were not calibrated to the right unit of measure, I found myself struggling to do basic tasks as a mechanic. In order to do the job I needed to do, I had to fill my toolbox with tools that corresponded to the right measurements.

The apostle Paul talks in II Corinthians about having the same kind of problem. Paul had struggled with using the wrong unit of measurement when sizing people up. You may remember that earlier in this chapter we talked about the Pharisees and their struggle to accept Jesus because He made them face their imperfection. Paul started out his career as a notable Pharisee. In those days his name was Saul. The Bible tells us that he was so upset about the person and message of Jesus that he hunted down believers "everywhere" and put them in jail (Acts 8:3). He even went so far as to be instrumental in the murder of one of the church's first pastors (Acts 7:58).

But a time came where God confronted Saul and, as a result, Saul became a believer in Jesus Christ. Afterward, his name was changed to Paul. Paul's mission efforts would make him one of the most influential figures in the early church, and the Bible itself is covered with Paul's fingerprints as God allowed him to pen the majority of the books in the New Testament. Paul realized that when he was a Pharisee, the way he "measured" people was wrong. His standard of measurement was faulty. Now, as a believer in Jesus Christ, he was retooling his measuring "equipment."

> *2 Corinthians 5:16–17 (NLT)*
> *16 So __we have stopped evaluating others from a human point of view__. At one time we thought of Christ merely from a human point of view. How differently we know him now! 17 This means that anyone who belongs to Christ has become a new person. The old life is gone; a new life has begun!*
> *[emphasis added]*

Paul said, in effect, "The way I used to measure or evaluate people—the human measurement system—ultimately doesn't work. I'm adopting a new system of measurement—God's."

Keith struggled to give Cynthia the acceptance she needed because Keith was still stuck evaluating her from his human system of measurement. According to his measurements she was lacking in many different areas, and this inspired him to share with her all the areas in which she needed to improve. Paul, in contrast, encourages us as believers to stop evaluating others with human measurements, and start evaluating people the way God does. I want to finish this chapter out by contrasting the human standard of measurement with God's standard of measurement.

How Did I Get Off-Track? Where Does A Failed "Standard Of Measurement" Come From?

Parents (Or The Way You Grew Up)

As Keith and I talked about his critical nature towards Cynthia, it was obvious that he was still hearing in his own mind the critical voices of his parents. They had spent years making him feel like he would never be good enough. The result was that he developed a faulty way to measure himself and others. Perhaps you can relate. Things as simple as which way the toilet paper roll is installed in the bathroom or how the toothpaste is squeezed to things as complex as how we spend our time or show our affection are often learned from the people around us as we grew up.

There's nothing wrong with our parents teaching us how to take on tasks and challenges, and even in having certain ways of doing things. What is not okay is when parents communicate that when things aren't done exactly "their way," the other person is bad or defective. This message, like a seed in the potting soil of a young child's heart will eventually grow into a standard of measurement that no one — including them — will ever live up to.

"Beth! Get up here right now!"

Lana, Beth's mom was accustomed to using her "yelling voice" to express her displeasure with Beth, and, at the moment, she was in rare form.

When Beth arrived atop the stairs, Lana let loose. "Where is your umbrella?"

Beth looked perplexed. "It's right there, mom… by the front door."

"That's right!" Lana said. "And do you have any idea why that's making me angry?"

"Because… Oh, right. Sorry. I forget that you don't want it inside when it's wet. I'll put it outside. Sorry." Beth replied.

Lana still towered above her daughter, intimidating the young girl with her size and body language. "I swear… you can't do anything right. I ask you to do one simple thing: keep the wet umbrella outside, and you can't even do that. It's just like I was telling your father, it's like you can't obey us. If you can't get over this selfish, careless streak, I won't know what to do with you when you get older. Guess you'll just have to figure it out on your own."

Beth eventually grew up and married a wonderful man. They both tried very hard to work through the challenges they experienced in their marriage, but when they came to see me Beth was on the verge of a breakdown. She lived in a world where no one was good enough. She would never be good enough, her husband would never be good enough, her kids would never be good enough... you get the point. As a result, the world was a very depressing place for Beth. Everywhere she looked she saw failure.

Beth was struggling with a standard of measure that she inherited from her parents. It was very hard for her to see the good in situations or in other people when her mother's voice echoed loudly in her ears, fatalistically pointing to the failure points in everything. This "inherited" standard of measure cost Beth dearly. It was this "voice of failure" that kept her from being able to enjoy her small group at church, her community of potential friends at work, and—ultimately—her marriage.

Pains And Insecurities

What was the deal with Beth's parents? Why did they have problems accepting their child? Were they just evil people? No. The reason they struggled with how they "measured" their daughter had to do with their insecurities. Beth's parents were very worried that they might not be raising their daughter right. Whenever Beth didn't do something the "right" way, they felt that there must be something wrong with them. When they sensed that they weren't doing a good enough job at parenting, they adjusted their measurements to force Beth to do better. The problem was that every time they adjusted their measurements, their standards became harder for Beth to meet.

Often parents will say that they are toughest on the child that is most like them. Why? Because our own insecurities play a large part in how we measure other people. In our story about Keith and Cynthia at the beginning of this chapter, we said that Keith's biggest problem was not Cynthia's imperfection, but his own. The true motivator behind Keith's unwillingness to accept Cynthia's behavior was his own unwillingness to accept his own behavior. He could not look at himself without feeling insecure, and as a result, he made Cynthia feel insecure also.

Our pain also has something to do with this measurement process. If you have been through a very painful experience before, especially one that involves relationships, it will be very difficult not to measure the world differently as a result of your experience. I often see this with individuals who are entering into a second marriage after the first ended in infidelity or abuse. The way these individuals measure their new spouse is often impacted by the pain they endured with their first spouse. It's very difficult not to let yesterday's pain change the way you evaluate people.

Many well-intentioned people struggle with the forces of personal pain and insecurity. One of the most difficult aspects of these problems is that people who are dealing with them often work very hard to appear as if nothing is wrong. Just like Beth's mother appears to be tough and put together, many individuals who are fighting off personal pain get labeled as being "harsh" or "unfeeling." The truth is that they feel very deeply. Often the harshness you see or hear is just the overflow of what they direct at themselves.

Selfishness

Sometimes the reason we measure people according to our own human standards is simply that we want people to be like us. In Psalms and Proverbs, the Bible refers to a type of person called a "fool." This person acts like there is no God (Psalm 14:1), and as a result lives to please himself. Since his life is built on meeting his own desires and standards, he doesn't much like it when other people won't get with the program. These individuals can't handle dealing with authority, and don't like getting close to other people unless the other person will focus solely on meeting their needs. Their standard of measure is a moving target, because his or her whims change from day to day.

You may know someone like this. They spend their life chasing "what they want," but they never truly get there. As a result, they are often disappointed with everyone. In terms of relationships they are "users." They are always looking for the person that will fulfill their needs and get them where they want to be. The people closest to these "fools" get that they will never be good enough for them. Eventually, people in close relationships with fools come to the realization that the best thing they can do is stop trying to do everything their way and let them experience the reality of life—they will never get exactly what they want.

The very fact that you are taking the time to read a book like this makes me think that you are probably not in the category of people we just talked about. You obviously care about what God has to say about relationships, or you wouldn't care about what this book has to say about your marriage. But let's face it… there's a little bit of this kind of selfishness in all of us. It may not dominate our lives and turn us into "fools," but it may cause us to act foolish sometimes. In those moments, when we see ourselves as doing things right and we're annoyed that other people won't do things "our way," we often end up doing or saying things that are out of character and hurtful. Our standard of measurement gets messed up and we start treating people foolishly.

How Can I Get Back On Track?
How Can I Accept My Spouse?

If you have been struggling with mis-measuring your spouse and need to recalibrate to God's standard of measurement, be encouraged. It can be done. There is one major realization you will have to adopt if you want to start measuring yourself and your spouse God's way. That realization is this:

My spouse and I are imperfect people and always will be. God loves us anyway.

If you can truly adopt the truth of this statement, you can measure your spouse God's way. If you take "perfect" off the table, and realize that part of being human is not doing everything right, you have the potential to see the good in yourself and in your spouse. Keith and Cynthia, the couple we talked about at the beginning of the chapter, both experienced new life in their relationship when they were willing to accept and embrace the imperfection in their home. Cynthia had experienced her own personal struggle with trying to be perfect, and when she saw how freeing it was for Keith to embrace his imperfection, she worked hard to do the same. Their inability to accept each other disappeared.

Keith and Cynthia noticed other benefits as well. Their new ability to measure themselves and others using God's standard of measure didn't just help their marriage, it helped them as parents as well. They were able to be more patient and compassionate not only with each other but also with their children. Their relationships in their church and local community seemed more vibrant and warm. The demands of perfection had clearly kept them from opening up as individuals and getting close to others.

You can experience the same kind of transformational growth Keith and Cynthia experienced. The best place to start is at the foot of Jesus' cross. When we came to faith, we realized that we were imperfect and needed rescuing. We asked God to forgive us for our imperfection and make us his child. At that moment we realized that our imperfection was not too great to keep us from being accepted. The key now is for you to embrace these truths again and apply them to your relationships.

POSTSCRIPT:
ACCEPTING A HURTFUL SPOUSE

You may be struggling to deal with this idea of seeing the good in your spouse if your spouse's "bad" side has caused you a lot of pain. Choosing to accept your spouse for who they are doesn't mean that you ignore or enable their bad behavior. In Hebrews 12:6, the apostle Paul tells us that God lets us experience the consequences of our bad choices *because* he loves and accepts us. God views the if-then nature of behavior and consequences as a normal part of relationship.

The key is that while God lets us experience the outcome of our bad choices, He still loves and accepts us. You can do this for your spouse. You don't have to ignore the things they do wrong, and you don't have to pretend everything is okay. Just to be clear, loving and accepting someone is not the same as protecting them from the consequences of their behavior. In the story of the prodigal son in Luke 15, the father did not go chasing after the son when he left. When the son eventually returned, he did not restore the inheritance that his son squandered. He could not. Those were the consequences of his son's rebellion. However, his spirit of acceptance allowed him to celebrate when his son "came to his senses" (Luke 15:17, 20).

I'm well aware that someone may be reading this chapter after having their marriage end as a result of their spouse's rebellion. Like the father in the prodigal son narrative, you may not be able to restore the relationship your spouse squandered, even if they were to "return" with repentance.

However, like the father, you can celebrate when and if your spouse chooses to turn from their foolishness and live for God. Again, you can always accept your spouse; you cannot always restore them. It's God's job to restore — in His way and in His timing.

Dear God,
Thank you for accepting me, and for paying for my imperfection. It's difficult to come to terms with my own imperfection, and sometimes that makes it difficult to deal with my spouse's problems. Help me to receive Your grace for myself, and extend Your grace to them. I know I can do that in Your power.

Chapter 7

YOUR SPOUSE NEEDS YOUR RESPECT

Joey and Melody seem to have a perfect marriage. The other couples in their small group at church look up to them as examples of a healthy relationship. In fact, the pastor has Joey and Melody on his "short list" of people that he can count on to help if needed with just about anything. Their can-do attitude made them fixtures in the PTA and in the neighborhood in which they lived. Looking from the outside in, Joey and Melody seem to have the kind of marriage most people dream about, but they know better.

The truth is, Joey and Melody live on a constant roller coaster of highs and lows, and the roller coaster seems to have a mind of its own. For their part, they do a good job at publicly showing the "highs," and (usually) keeping the "lows" private.

One night, however, the fight between them became so intense that the screaming from inside their house was audible to the neighbors. As others in their cul-de-sac stared through their windows, Joey stomped out of the house slamming the door behind him and yelling things at Melody you wouldn't want your kids to hear. Meanwhile, Melody grabs an armful of random objects within arm's reach, and throws them with surprising force at Joey's automobile as he makes a rapid exit.

Joey knows, Melody knows, and now the neighbors know that something is really wrong here. As Joey sits alone in a parking lot trying to let off steam and calm down, he asks himself, *Why does this keep happening to us? We're good people; why can't we get along?*

Meanwhile, Melody is struggling with the same sort of questions. *Why would he say those things to me? Then again, why would I throw my favorite umbrella stand at his car? Why do we act so crazy? Why do we get so mad? We love each other… why does this keep happening?*

In order to answer that question, we need to rewind the tape a bit. Earlier that day, Joey and Melody had been doing very well together. Joey had called Melody at lunch time just to see how she was doing, and they had a very enjoyable conversation. Then, coming home, Joey was bursting at the seams with good news. He had a big surprise for Melody, and he couldn't wait to see how happy she was when he told her about it.

"Guess what!" he said to Melody as he burst through the door.

"What?" Melody said half-heartedly. She had been through an incredibly tiring day already, and was not feeling very compatible at the moment with whatever energy trip her husband was apparently on.

"We're going to Hawaii!" he shouted.

Melody was shocked. "When?"

"That's the best part! Friday!" Joey beamed a genuine smile from ear to ear as he expectantly waited for his wife's response. But as he looked into Melody's eyes, he didn't see overwhelming joy. He saw panic.

"We can't go to Hawaii on Friday!" she shouted. "We've made no plans to go out of town. Who would we ask to watch the kids? They've got soccer, and music lessons, and the swim meet—oh, the swim meet… we would miss that, too… There's just no option then. We can't go. Why would you go and do something like this without asking me first? Why didn't you talk to me about this? This is what you *always* do. Why can't you think things through before you spend a fortune on tickets that we can't use? Why don't you give me a chance to be a part of the process? Geez, I can't win with you."

Joey was crestfallen. After all, he had attempted to do something nice for his wife, only to have her act as though he had done something terribly wrong. The moment of depression lasted briefly though, because about two seconds after his wife finished talking, he became intensely angry. This wasn't his fault, after all. He deserved to be treated better than this.

"So this is my fault?" he asked indignantly. "Fine! Be mad at me. I'll go to Hawaii by myself, and I'll have a good time. It'll be better than staying here with a control freak like you!"

For about an hour, Joey continued to tell his wife that the problem of the Hawaii tickets rested on her shoulders. She was too inflexible. She had never given his trip a chance. He reminded her that they hadn't discussed possible solutions for childcare or how they might deal with missing the swim meet. Then, when that didn't work, he resorted to calling her names again, telling her that she was a nag who somehow delighted in being miserable and made everyone around her feel miserable, too.

Meanwhile, Melody continued to berate her husband for making a big decision like this without consulting her. She began to insist that he did this on purpose. Maybe he meant to make plans that would force her to miss something that mattered to her. In addition, Melody was keenly aware of the fact that her husband often felt that she was not spontaneous enough — that she micromanaged things like vacations. "Just let it happen — be spontaneous!" he would say. Spontaneity was never Melody's strong suit, and she felt that Joey couldn't accept that about her. Now she was yelling at Joey things like, "You did this on purpose! You're trying to *make* me be spontaneous. Well, it won't work!"

Joey and Melody were usually good about shielding their children from seeing or being involved in their conflict, but tonight wasn't one of their better nights. At this point, Joey and Melody are yelling, the kids are crying, and nothing seems to be moving in a positive direction.

That's when Joey said, "Alright, that's it. I'm out of here!"

Melody quickly replied, "Oh, no you don't! I'm not letting you leave until we talk this out." Melody then stood in the doorway blocking her husband from walking out of the house.

Joey chuckled, remembering that there was a separate door leading to the garage. *She can't block both doors,* he thought. The following moments of Joey and Melody's fight would have worked well as fodder for a television comedy.

For two minutes, two grown people ran back and forth between the doors of the house as Joey tried to make his getaway, and Melody tried to force him to stay. From this angle, it seems humorous, but to Joey and Melody it was serious business. Finally, Joey wrangled his way out of the door and made it to his car. Shouting angrily, he unceremoniously crammed himself into his car and peeled out of the driveway. He sped away so quickly that he barely realized that his wife was throwing objects at his car.

I know what you're thinking. *This couple has issues.* But the truth is that most of the time Joey and Melody get along. That's why fights like this one are so confusing. This couple loves each other and God. They are absolutely committed to each other, and they know that relationships require sacrifice and kindness. Usually they do pretty well at getting along, but the good moments are hard to celebrate when the bad moments can be so distressing.

If Joey and Melody were reading this book, they might be checking off the list as they go through the last few chapters: Trust? Yes. They definitely trust each other. Being there for each other? They do really well at that. (Unless they're in the middle of a big fight.) Comforting each other? They do a great job at that. And as far as supporting each other goes, they've done a good job at being there for each other when they take on life's big challenges. But this chapter is about respect, and that's where they have a lot of growing to do.

In this chapter, I would like to walk you through the three crucial respect points that are necessary in any close relationship. My hope is to use the story of Joey and Melody to illustrate these three ideas and help you understand how honoring your spouse can be the way to exit the "roller coaster."

1. RESPECT YOUR SPOUSE'S UNIQUENESS.

Uniqueness is the hallmark of God's creative genius. Your relationship is full of unique characteristics. There is no one quite like you, and there is no one exactly like your spouse. The two of you are unique, and together you form an especially unique relationship. But unique is just a nice word for different, and we all know that differences can cause problems in relationships.

When you were first dating, you were keenly aware that you and your significant other were different in many ways. When we're in that early stage of our relationship, those differences are easy to see as cute or quirky. Then after you've been married for a while, those same differences may seem irritating, annoying, or problematic. For instance, perhaps in your relationship there is one person who doesn't mind complaining with gusto when service at a restaurant is bad, while the other would prefer not to "make waves." Maybe one of you would prefer to be "on the go" much of the time, while the other would prefer to stay at home. It could be that one of you loves and thrives on change, while the other would be completely content if the furniture were never rearranged.

Lots of Christian marriage books, seminars, and materials spend a great deal of time detailing the differences between men and women. Sometimes these differences are universal and important to understand. Other times, these differences are overgeneralized and cause more confusion than help. Here's the bottom line—men and women are different, and that's important to understand. *More important*, though, is understanding that your spouse is different from *everyone* else. In many ways, your spouse will not fit any particular mold, because he or she is unique. The trick is learning to honor their uniqueness—to show them respect.

Compatible or Special?

Our culture has a compatibility hang-up. Commercials flash across television screens promising to connect single individuals to other people with whom they are significantly compatible. Couples are encouraged to find a "match" that shares many common interests and goals. As a result of this compatibility craziness, people are walking away from marriages today because they feel as though they accidentally married a person who is not enough like them. "Our personalities just don't match," I hear often. "We married too fast without getting to know each other" is another one I hear a lot. It's as if we've forgotten that uniqueness is part of how God makes things *special*.

You and your spouse may be extremely different, but that doesn't mean that your relationship is doomed to failure. The opposite is true.

> *Matthew 19:4–6 (NLT)*
> *4 "Haven't you read the Scriptures?" Jesus replied. "They record that from the beginning 'God made them male and female.' 5 And he said, 'This explains why a man leaves his father and mother and is joined to his wife, and the two are united into one.' 6 Since they are no longer two but one, let no one split apart what God has joined together."*

In Matthew 19, Jesus shares what marriage is all about. He starts by saying that God created "male and female." Notice that Jesus' first statement about how God created marriage emphasizes a difference and not a similarity.

Notice that Jesus doesn't then say:

"This explains why a man interviews all the available dating options to determine which is most compatible with his way of life..."

"This explains why a man and woman can marry as long as their personality inventories match well..."

"This explains why a man and woman determine to marry after living together long enough to see if they are a 'good fit'..."

Nope. There is no compatibility talk here, just the voice of Jesus reminding us that when two unique people choose to join their lives together, God goes about the important business of creating a unique new entity—a marriage "joined" by God and characterized by differences that bear evidence of His design.

Now, let's go back to Joey and Melody. Joey knows that he and Melody approach the world from different angles. He handles change easily, and loves to do things on the "spur of the moment." When the Hawaii trip opportunity came up, he jumped on it because that's what *he wanted to do.* He knew that Melody doesn't approach life the way that he does, but he was tired of her being different than him. *She should have to compromise a little,* he thought. *That's what marriage is all about. Anyhow, I know she'll enjoy the trip.* The sad truth is that Joey knew before he bought the plane tickets that Melody might really struggle with an unplanned trip like this.

Joey and Melody both do this. They know the areas in which they are different than each other, and in their own ways they continue to try to *make the other person be more like them.* Melody has spent countless hours trying to make Joey become more organized, and Joey has never given up trying to make Melody be more carefree. This difference and many others often create conflict for Joey and Melody because they don't look at their differences as things that make each other special anymore. They look at the differences as inconvenient and agitating.

Think about this. How is your spouse different from you? In what ways is God expressing his creativity in your life by allowing your spouse to be different from you? Take this opportunity to reacquaint yourself with the positive side of your spouse's approach to life. Like Joey and Melody, you have a choice. Are the differences you and your spouse experience a sign that you're not compatible, or are they a sign that your relationship is special… unique… God-designed?

The traditional marriage vows include a rarely used but beautiful word. "Cherish." When we promise "to love and to cherish" our spouse, we are promising to honor the unique God-designed person that they are, and to continue to view them as *special* even after the new has worn off. Are you cherishing your spouse? Sure, they are different than you. That's the point… that's what makes your relationship special.

2. RESPECT YOUR SPOUSE'S INTENTIONS.

Joey would have been much better off if he had not booked the Hawaii trip without consulting Melody, but at the deepest level, he meant well. He wanted to take a trip that would be enjoyable and exciting for him *and* Melody. He wanted her to be able to relax and enjoy some down time. While he may have been trying to broaden Melody's horizons by booking the trip on the spur of the moment, he had no *evil* intentions. He meant to do the right thing.

The hardest pill for Joey to swallow in this interaction was that his wife could not see his good intentions. She could not identify with the fact that he was trying to do something positive. He knew her well enough to understand why she decided she didn't want to go on the trip. What he did not understand is why the woman he loved couldn't believe the best about him, and instead assumed the worst.

Why does it make us feel so desperate when our spouse can't respect our good intentions? I think there are two reasons.

Because we are trying.

I don't know anyone who begins the day by waking up and wishing to be a failure. Most of us desperately want to be successful. We want to succeed in our marriage, in our efforts as parents, in our occupation, and in many other areas. Despite the fact that we are human and we all have areas in which we fail, we *try* to do a good job.

So when our spouse doesn't recognize our efforts, we feel that there is no point—we feel that all of our energy is wasted. Pause for a moment and think about your spouse. They do try, don't they? Perhaps they fail... but they try.

Right now, my three-year-old daughter desperately wants to be able to do the things that her big sister can do. Since our eight-year-old is doing lots of writing in school, our youngest wants to write, too. My wife has given her letters to trace and write, and she's doing remarkably well for her age. Can you imagine the outcome if I were to pick up the sheet of paper on which my little girl had been tracing letters and remark, "How sloppy! You can't expect to get anywhere in life if you can't learn to write any better than this! If you can't shape up, you should just give up." This sort of discouragement might be just enough to convince my daughter to walk away from a very worthwhile endeavor.

Your spouse, much like my little three-year-old, is doing something unfamiliar, difficult, and intimidating—trying to learn how to be a good spouse. You will watch them grow in some areas and become proficient, while in other areas they may still struggle. Don't discourage them! They are trying. If you convince them that their trying isn't good enough, they may be inspired to walk away from their efforts instead of redoubling them.

Because we care about our spouse's
   opinion of ourselves.

Everyday before I leave the house in the morning, I look in the bathroom mirror to make sure that I'm presentable. I want to make sure that I'm okay before I head out to face the world. In many ways, my wife Wendy is a different kind of mirror in my life. Throughout our married life, I have often listened to Wendy's view of me — her thoughts about my strengths and weaknesses — as a way of evaluating how I'm doing as a spouse and as a person.

Why would I do that? Because I care about how Wendy views me. That's the nature of a love relationship. Part of becoming close to another person and developing a trusting love relationship is choosing to value their opinion. Think about it. When you were dating your spouse, how much of your conversations at that point revolved around sharing each other's opinions? You cared about how they liked the movie you just watched, the clothes you wore that evening, or the meal you were sharing. As you became closer, you became more interested in how they felt about your family, your friends, your occupation, and your habits. Now, many of those questions have been answered. But make no mistake about it… there is one question you and your spouse will continue asking each other for the rest of your marriage, and that question is: "How do you feel about me?"

Whether you're a man or a woman, you know that when your spouse communicates their approval of you, it makes your day. Sure, most of us are not good at *accepting* compliments, but all of us are good at *hearing* them. Ladies, when your husband tells you that you are the most beautiful woman in the world, you may demure and let the compliment roll off, but you know that deep in your heart you heard what he said, and you needed to hear it. Guys, when your wife tells you that you're the only man in the world for her and that she thinks you're a stud, you may not be comfortable accepting that compliment, but down deep you know that what she said made you feel ten stories tall.

It's true that your opinion of your spouse should not be the only thing that communicates self-worth to them. But what if it were? If you were the only "mirror" in your spouse's life, how would they feel about themselves? If you were the only source of personal reflection for him or her, what would they believe about their worth?

Putting It Together

When we give our spouse the "benefit of the doubt" that they have good intentions, even when those intentions don't materialize perfectly, we show them that we know they are trying. More than that, we inspire them to see how worthwhile they really are. As a "mirror" in their life, we reflect a view that showcases the best part of them, not the worst. We encourage them to keep trying to turn their good intentions into reality, rather than rub their nose in their failures. We all fail. The question is, who will be in your spouse's corner? Who will see the best in them? The answer should be you.

3. RESPECT YOUR SPOUSE'S LIMITS.

Before this chapter closes, I want to do my best to explain why things between Joey and Melody managed to get so crazy. Think for a moment about all of the things that Joey and Melody did during this fight that they would *never do* if they had been thinking straight. They would not have allowed this issue to get so out of hand. They would not have fought in front of their kids. Joey wouldn't have been so determined to escape the house, and Melody wouldn't have blocked him from leaving. Given a day or so to get some perspective on this fight, both Joey and Melody are going to have some sincere regrets. Why would this couple act so out of character?

At my home, we have a new pet. We adopted a very sweet long-haired Jack Russell Terrier named Dori. Since our little girls had never lived with a dog in the house, we did our best to try to teach them how to treat a dog. They are very loving little girls, but we knew it was a good idea to explain the basics. One of the first things we shared with them about Dori is that although she is a loving, sweet, gentle dog, if you back her into a corner, she'll snap at you. In this way, many of us share something in common with Dori. We are loving, gentle, kind people, but when we feel as though we are backed into a corner, we flip into fight-or-flight mode, and we begin to behave out of character.

Joey and Melody are great at pushing each other's buttons until they get to that fight-or-flight place. For instance, what really gets Melody desperate is when Joey tries to walk away. When Joey said, "Alright! That's it. I'm out of here!" Melody panicked. Deep in her heart, alarm bells went off and she felt like somehow she was losing Joey. Logically, she knows that Joey will come back. He will calm down and eventually he'll walk back through the door and they'll both apologize to each other. They will move on. But logic doesn't prevail in moments like this. For Joey, seeing Melody pursue him pushes his buttons and makes him panic. When she starts to "go after him," he feels as though things are out of control and he has to get out. Logically, he knows that his wife is not going to do him any major harm, but logic doesn't prevail when we're stuck in fight-or-flight.

Often when I work with couples, one or both individuals will say something like "we sure know how to push each other's buttons." That's just another way of saying "we sure know how to make each other feel desperate." If you know how to push your spouse's buttons, then I have good news for you. It means that you know what makes your spouse feel desperate, and now you have the opportunity to use this power for good instead of evil. This whole fight could have easily been reduced to a simple discussion, if this couple simply would have respected each other's limits. Make no mistake about it—they know what those limits are. From start to finish, they were pushing each other into corners.

You and your spouse both have limits. God engineered you that way. Like a defined property line, these limits in many ways define the territory of who you are. When your spouse crosses that line, or you cross theirs, craziness ensues. Some of the "lines" in the relationship are universals set by God. For instance, there are lines that should never be crossed in any marriage relationship, like the line of infidelity or the line of abuse. God has clearly stated that crossing these lines violates the marriage and gives grounds for divorce. Joey and Melody won't be crossing any of those lines. They respect God's Word and they plan to follow God's rules for the relationship. It's the fainter lines that they easily cross. Lines like, "Please don't walk away from me without reassuring me that you will come back and talk to me about this." Or, "Please don't yell at me. It makes me feel hurt and desperate."

If you know what pushes your spouse's buttons, you know where the lines are.

> *Ephesians 5:21 (NLT)*
> *21 And further, submit to one another out of reverence for Christ.*

When God tells us to put each other first, inherent in that statement is that we must respect each other's limits. Putting the other person first logically means that we must learn to care about the lines that define who they are.

How many times have you had to apologize for doing or saying things that really pushed your spouse's buttons? Wouldn't it be incredible if you could avoid going to that desperate place with your spouse? In the next part of this chapter, I'd like to share two key thoughts that can help you respect your spouse's limits and avoid pushing their buttons.

Understand the law of "runners and chasers."

There are two kinds of desperate people in this world: runners and chasers. Somehow runners seem to always marry chasers. Runners are intimidated by the craziness of the fight and often leave when things get heated. Instead of facing the problem head-on, a runner will "go behind a wall" by being unresponsive or absent in order to restore calm. Runners say things like, "I'm not having this discussion." Or, "That's it. I'm out of here." Or, "Drop it! I don't want to talk about it anymore."

Chasers, on the other hand, deal with problems by attacking them head-on. When a chaser gets desperate, he or she keeps thinking, "If I could only get them to listen to me, they'd fix this." Getting a chaser to stop talking and leave you alone in the middle of a desperate moment of conflict is not likely. They are on task. Somehow, some way, they will get you to hear what they have to say and do something about it.

The law of runners and chasers works like this: *the faster a runner runs, the faster a chaser chases, and the faster a chaser chases, the faster a runner runs.* This is why things get so crazy for Joey and Melody. When Joey gets desperate and goes behind a wall, this makes Melody panic. She's a chaser, so the way she deals with Joey's wall is to run after it with a battering ram. The more Melody tries to tear down Joey's walls, the more walls Joey puts up. As a result they both become more desperate.

If you and your spouse have ever lived this, you know there is no terminal velocity for a fight that has the *runner and chaser* dynamic. If one of you is determined to walk away from a fight, and the other is determined to chase and pursue until there is some resolution, things can get crazy very fast. Part of moving forward in your relationship is learning what part you play in this cycle. If your spouse is a runner—if they go behind walls during conflict—ask yourself this question: "Am I inspiring them to go behind a wall because they feel that I am chasing them?" If your spouse chases you, ask yourself, "Am I intimidating them by putting up walls?"

The Joey's and Melody's of the world could experience incredible forward movement in their relationship if they were willing to recognize the part they both play in the craziness of their conflict. If Joey could recognize that his insistence on walking away was inspiring Melody to block him, and if Melody could recognize that her insistence on blocking Joey makes him want to walk away, they could make the *choice* to get off the roller coaster.

Don't try to fight an emotional battle with logic.
Reassure first, reason second.

So, what should Joey and Melody do? First, they need to recognize that the battlefield of this fight is emotional, not logical. If logic was the main force in this conflict, Melody would have logically seen Joey's good intentions, and Joey would have logically realized why Melody couldn't go on this trip. Logic didn't bring this fight to crazytown. Emotion did. So when Joey tries to explain logically to Melody that this trip is good for them, and *is possible*, Melody refuses to hear any of it. When Melody tries to use logic to persuade Joey that the trip would cause big problems and *isn't possible*, Joey has no intention of listening either. You must remember this *it is completely pointless to fight an emotional battle with logic.* As a matter of fact, it's somewhat like trying to fight a raging fire with gasoline.

Thousands of individuals across this country are deathly afraid of flying in an airplane. Their fear should teach us something. For decades, statistics have revealed that it is safer per mile and per minute to fly in an airplane than it is to drive in a car, so no one should be afraid of flying if fear can be conquered with logic alone. But it can't. Our deepest emotions don't have to make sense to be real. Your spouse's experience in your relationship is incredibly real to them, whether or not you can prove they are wrong. So don't come to a conflict armed with all the reasons they should view the world from your perspective — it won't work.

Like math, there is an order of operations to dealing with our spouse's emotional anxiety and pain. It starts by meeting them where they are. It starts when you are willing to understand the emotional place in which they are stuck. That requires you to do two things: listen and care. In order to meet them where they are in their emotional struggle, you must be willing to hear them out, and express care and concern — whether or not you see things their way.

By fully identifying with what your spouse is going through, you will have given them *emotional comfort*. Then and *only then* will you have the necessary buy-in from them to give *logical comfort*. If you're a parent, you understand this. When your children were very small, you could not comfort them with logic, because they were not yet ready to hear logical arguments and process them. They were too young. You comforted them with your presence, with your hugs, and with your words of love. In short, *you reassured your child everything would be okay.*

Too many times we don't realize that our spouse is often in need of the same type of comfort. Sure, they're old enough to process logical insight, but often they will be too hurt to hear and process logical arguments. Just as your child needed your emotional comfort when logic would do no good, your spouse will need your *reassurance* when things start to get crazy. Bring all your logic to the discussion later... later on you can try to sort the whole thing out by reasoning your way through it, but not while either of you are in a desperate place. *Reassure first; reason second.*

A NEXT LEVEL CHALLENGE

If you make the choice to understand your spouse's limits and respect them, you will find that your conflict is less difficult — that's a given, but there is one other huge benefit that will come along for the ride. The more you respect your spouse's limits, the closer your relationship can be. Here's the goal to which we should all aspire: once we know what those "lines" are in the relationship that we should not cross — those limits that our spouse should not be pushed beyond — we must become the guardians of the line. Instead of being the person who chooses to violate your spouse's boundaries, be that person who *guards* their boundaries. If you do that, you and your spouse will be inseparable. Why? Because that's the way God designed it to work.

Genesis 2:18 (NLT)
18 Then the Lord God said, "It is not good for the man to be alone. I will make a helper who is just right for him."

A WORD OF CONCLUSION

Your spouse was designed in the image of God. Regardless of how you feel about him or her in the midst of your worst fights, God loves them intensely. In fact, God would have sent his Son to die for your spouse even if they were the only person on the face of the earth. Your wife, sir, is a daughter of the living God. Ma'am, your husband is one of God's precious sons. God has asked you to put them first. Are you okay with that?

Disclaimer:
As I stated earlier in this chapter, the Bible is clear that there are certain actions that have the destructive power necessary to end a marriage. If your spouse is cheating on you or abusing you, this chapter was not designed for you. In this moment, you need to respect yourself by getting help from a trusted source as soon as possible.

Dear God,
Sometimes it's hard to put my spouse first. It's especially hard when we aren't getting along, and when I feel desperate. Help me to remember that even when I am desperate, You are there to comfort me. Help me to extend Your comfort and reassurance to my spouse when they are desperate. Don't let me be a "button-pusher" — let me be the person who "guards the line" by honoring my spouse.

Chapter 8

YOUR SPOUSE NEEDS TO BE DESIRED

I'm not typically one for fanciful thinking, but for the sake of making a point, assume for a moment that you have discovered a magic lamp that—true to the cliché—contains a genie who will grant a wish for you. Let's keep it simple for now—one wish. Imagine the genie asks you the question you've been waiting for: "What do you want?" Remember, you can wish for *anything*. What would your answer be? Got it? Good. Now, think about what your answer would have been a month ago, a year ago, or ten years ago. Would those answers be different?

One of the reasons that relationships struggle over time is because our "wish list" changes. Think about this. When you were dating and overcome with the hormonal euphoria of the new relationship, you might have answered the genie by wishing for *what you have now*. You might have wished that you could be married to the person you loved and have the ability to build a life together. But, if we were honest, we'd have to admit that once we attained our goal of capturing the heart of the one we love, we moved on to new things to "wish" for.

Your spouse will be very good at noticing when your "wish list" changes. You'll hear them vocalize the fact that they are aware that other things are becoming more important than them. Maybe they'll recognize that your friends or family seem to have a greater place of importance in your life than they do, or they'll feel that your job or hobbies have forced them to take a back seat. Sometimes, they will even feel like some particular aspect of the marriage relationship itself is more important than them. This would be the case with the wife that announces, "All he wants me for is sex!" Or with the husband who barks out, "All I am to her is a paycheck!"

Our desires in life can so easily shift. Once we have something, it's almost second nature to let our desire for that thing diminish. Think about the last bright and shiny thing you just had to have. Perhaps it was a new car, a new house, or something smaller like a new outfit or a new cell phone. Isn't it interesting that during the thrill of the chase — those moments when you're doing anything you can think of to attain the object of your desire — your entire focus centers on that one thing? Notice how easily our desire wanes over time once we have the item.

The new car eventually becomes just "the car," the cell phone that you just had to have eventually becomes "the phone you can't wait to upgrade," and the dress that defined your sense of style becomes "just another outfit" in your closet. The bottom line: the more we feel we *have* something, the easier it is to *want it less*. Isn't it fair to say that this happens in our marriages as well? Up until the "I do's" were spoken and the rings were exchanged, we wanted nothing more than to spend our lives with our sweetheart. Once the ink is dry on the marriage certificate, we *have* that person. In fact, we have a lot of that person — every day. It's easy to want your spouse less just because you feel that you already have them.

THE TRADE-OFF

One of Satan's go-to methods for ruining people's lives is to get them to take God's biggest gifts for granted. By putting Adam and Eve in the Garden of Eden, God gave Adam and Eve a gift of inestimable worth. They were not living in the broken world we now face. They were experiencing God's best in every way before Satan showed up to cause trouble. *God* is in the business of giving huge gifts you *should* have. *Satan* is in the business of redirecting your attention to harmful (nevertheless, attractive) things you *shouldn't* have.

Read this narrative from Genesis, and notice that the very first thing Satan does is to focus Eve's attention on what she can't have.

> *Genesis 3:1–5 (NLT)*
> *The serpent was the shrewdest of all the wild animals the Lord God had made. One day he asked the woman, "Did God really say you must not eat the fruit from any of the*

trees in the garden?"
2 "Of course we may eat fruit from the trees in the garden,"
the woman replied. 3 "It's only the fruit from the tree in
the middle of the garden that we are not allowed to eat.
God said, 'You must not eat it or even touch it; if you do,
you will die.' "
4 "You won't die!" the serpent replied to the woman. 5 "God
knows that your eyes will be opened as soon as you eat it,
and you will be like God, knowing both good and evil."

God intended for Adam and Eve to have the beautiful gift of the Garden of Eden, but Satan was successful in getting this couple to take their focus off the gift and become consumed with something they weren't supposed to have. As a result, they lost God's gift. Time and again I have met with men who have lost the marriage that God gave them because Satan was successful in getting them to focus on another woman, or pornography, or some other attractive-but-harmful trap. Many times I have seen a woman squander the God-given beauty of her marriage because Satan was effective at getting her to focus on an old flame that was rekindled over social media or a guy at work who was a good listener and a shoulder to cry on.

I was recently meeting with a young man who lost his wife because of his addiction to pornography. He made a remark that will forever resonate with me. He said, "I had no idea how expensive this would be." I've often thought that perhaps that might be the sentiment of an older-and-wiser Adam and Eve. Despite God's warning, Satan's trap looked so available, enticing, and easy. Once they made the decision to pursue the wrong thing, they were faced with the reality of how expensive their decision would be. God's gifts are so easy to lose when we make the choice to pursue what we were not intended to have.

CHOOSING THE GIFT

So how do you avoid losing God's best in your life? How do you keep God's gifts and avoid Satan's traps? Two words: personal choice. You need to make a decision here and now that you are going to focus on what God wants you to have. My dad likes to put it this way, "It's impossible to lure away a contented person." No one can make you focus on what you have, and not even Satan can force you to focus on what you don't have. That's your decision. What will you dwell on in life?

> *Proverbs 5:18–19 (NLT)*
> 18 **Let your wife be a fountain** *of blessing for you.*
> **Rejoice in the wife of your youth.**
> 19 *She is a loving deer, a graceful doe.*
> **Let her breasts satisfy you always.**
> *May you* **always be captivated by her love.**
> *[emphasis added]*

Look at all the words in this passage that speak of *your responsibility* in a marriage relationship. "*Let your wife*" or husband be a blessing for you. Make the choice to "*rejoice*" in your wife or husband. "*Let her*" or him satisfy you sexually. "*Be captivated*" by your spouse's love. If you want to receive God's best in your life and in your marriage, you must be intentional about keeping your spouse at the top of your wish list. It's often been said that greed is an overwhelming drive to have what you want, while contentment is a decision to want what you have. Where are you on this continuum? Is your life characterized by trying to have the things you want, or have you made the choice to want the things you have?

THREE KEYS TO MAKING THIS WORK

How do you make the decision to "want" your spouse? How does a person passionately pursue the heart of their spouse even as life threatens to reduce romance to the hum-drum rhythm of the everyday? In the rest of this chapter, I want to share with you three main keys to keeping your spouse at the top of your wish list. Use these thoughts to evaluate your heart toward your spouse today, and to calibrate your actions as you seek to help them feel desired in the future.

Keep the main thing the main thing. Distractions can destroy your future.

I cannot imagine a man in the history of the world that received more of God's favor than King David. God elevated David from his lowly post—watching sheep for the family—and made him the King of Israel. Along the way, God helped David kill a menacing giant and face the evil treachery of the old King of Israel (who didn't really want to be replaced). As King of Israel, David was very loved and respected. I don't think it's an overstatement to say that David was the greatest king Israel ever had.

But David would make a mistake that would cost him dearly for the rest of his life. David slept with another man's wife and had her husband killed to cover up his indiscretion. Here's the question that we have to answer: How could a person who *was* so devoted to God make such a big mistake? How does a person go from making great—perhaps God-directed—decisions, to doing something so foolish?

Maybe you've known someone in your life that has been in the same sort of situation. They seemed wise and godly, and you really believed that they were spiritually "bulletproof." You felt like they would be the last person to make a big moral mistake, but you were wrong. Perhaps you were bewildered by the discontinuity of what seemed like their genuine affection for God and their personal life choices which showed disregard for God. How do these things happen?

Distraction vs. Priority

Why did King David do such a foolish thing? He started treating *distractions like priorities* and *priorities like distractions*. Distractions are things in life I don't need to do. Priorities are just the opposite. Jot down a list of things you *must do* in life, and you have just made a list of your priorities. Now, if you make a list of things you would like to do but don't have to do, you will have itemized a number of distractions in your life. King David learned a lesson that perhaps you have learned as well: not keeping your priorities in check puts you on a very slippery slope.

The Bible helps us understand when David first started treating his priorities like distractions.

> *2 Samuel 11:1 (NLT)*
> *In the spring of the year, when kings normally go out to war, David sent Joab and the Israelite army to fight the Ammonites. They destroyed the Ammonite army and laid siege to the city of Rabbah. However, David stayed behind in Jerusalem.*

The Bible reminds us that at this time of the year it was "normal" for kings to go out to war. David has a choice between doing what kings are supposed to do (fighting alongside their army), or kicking around the palace while he lets his military officials handle the battle. The Bible is helping us make the distinction that at certain times in David's life, palace life was appropriate, but *during this season, it was a distraction.* David didn't *need* to be at the palace. He needed to be with his men leading them on to victory. He chose, rather, to do what he wanted to do instead of what he needed to do. Because he treated the distraction of palace life like a priority, he ended up treating the priority of God's calling as a leader in his life like a distraction. This placed David on shaky footing.

> *2 Samuel 11:2–4 (NLT)*
> *2 Late one afternoon, after his midday rest, David got out*

*of bed and was walking on the roof of the palace. As he
looked out over the city, he noticed a woman of unusual
beauty taking a bath. 3 He sent someone to find out who
she was, and he was told, "She is Bathsheba, the daughter
of Eliam and the wife of Uriah the Hittite." 4 Then David
sent messengers to get her; and when she came to the palace,
he slept with her...*

I don't think David planned to do this from the beginning.
It's not like David told his military leaders, "Hey guys, why
don't you go ahead and head out to the battlefields? I'll
stay behind and have an affair with a married woman." No,
it started with the distraction of palace life — something
innocent, but unnecessary. How many relationship-killing
behaviors and addictions start this way? At the beginning
of a downward spiral there is an innocent act, distraction, or preoccupation that sets a person on a slippery
slope. By the time the person realizes that they have
accommodated foolishness in their life they have made
significant — sometimes irreparable — mistakes.

Think for a moment about all of the innocent-but-
unnecessary distractions in our lives. Technology has
created these types of distractions at an alarming pace.
We have television sets, radios, mobile electronic devices,
the internet, social media, and a million other glowing,
beeping, vibrating, time-and-resource zapping sink holes
that threaten to put each of us on a slippery slope. I'm
certainly not arguing that all of these things should be
done away with, just as David was not expected to do
away with palace life. I'm setting forward the idea that

these distractions *must* take a back seat to our priorities. I'm suggesting that you be the manager of the distractions in your life instead of letting distractions manage you.

Recently, I was meeting my wife and kids at a restaurant for supper. I was there about ten minutes early, so while I waited for them I casually looked around observing the people in the restaurant. At several tables I noticed people weren't looking at each other. Instead they were looking down at their little mobile electronic devices, typing proficiently with their thumbs and stopping occasionally to take pictures of their "family night" for their favorite social media site. If families cannot even focus on each other across the table at a restaurant—*because of innocent-but-unnecessary distractions* — we should not be at all surprised that our families are falling apart at an alarming rate.

It's All In How You Do The Math

My wife has always been the financial wizard of our family. Being the more organized and analytical person in our relationship, she graciously accepted that responsibility at the beginning of our marriage. My wife is very aware when she "does the bills" that there are several things we *must* spend money on, and about a million things we *could* spend money on. The things we must purchase are "needs," and all the other things could be classified as "wants." There is no way that we can afford both. So my wife does the math this way—"needs" get the first money available. If "wants" are to be purchased, they must be purchased with what funds are left over after the needs are met.

Just like my wife and I will never have the finances to purchase everything we need *plus* everything we want, you will never have enough time to accommodate all of your priorities *plus* all of the attractive distractions in your life. It's all in how you do the math. If you want to have a successful life and a successful marriage, the innocent distractions in your life should get the leftovers. They should get the time that remains after all the priorities in your life have been adequately addressed.

If you like to watch TV or hang out on social media sites, make sure that every priority in your life has been adequately addressed before you spend your valuable time there. If you do the math right, you'll likely find that distractions get very little of your time, and become very manageable.

Gut-Check Time

What is distracting you from making your marriage a priority right now? Is your spouse getting your time "leftovers?" What distracts you from listening to your spouse? What keeps you from focusing on them the way you did when you were dating? What distractions are stealing away the time you have for communicating, doing things together, just hanging out, seriously making out, or having sex? This is a moment for some introspection — because distractions have the ability to rob you of life's greatest blessings. If you want your spouse to be at the top of your wish list, you must separate your priorities and your distractions and make the choice to put your priorities first.

Invest. Desire always follows investment.

A Tale of Two Oldsmobiles (A Purely Fictional Story)

It's 1986. A large U.S. home supply retailer holds a "neighbor sweepstakes." People who live next to each other are encouraged to enter the competition, and two of these neighbors will be fortunate enough to win beautiful brand new 1986 Oldsmobile sedans. These cars had everything you could hope for in a car at the time. Power everything, plush seats, a beautiful gold exterior with a cream-colored vinyl roof… these cars were awesome. When the drawing was held, the two guys who won had their pictures taken with the cars and drove them home.

One guy—we'll call him Bob—loved the car he won. Not one day passed that he didn't remember how fortunate he was to win such a wonderful prize. He never let anyone else drive his car. He always kept it spotless inside and out. Whenever there was a mechanical failure of any sort, he immediately had it repaired. Bob's Oldsmobile was his pride and joy.

His neighbor—we'll call him Jim—really loved his car, too… at first. Jim treated his new car kind of like "found money." He figured he was lucky to have it, but since he didn't pay anything for it, he didn't see any point in putting too much work into it. Eventually Jim got tired of the car, and gave it to his wife to drive. Eventually, she passed it down to their son. After years of abuse, Jim's car was starting to show its age.

Ten years from the date of the original contest, Bob's car sits in his carport, glistening in the afternoon sun. To Bob, his car is worth more now than the day he won it. Next door, a vehicle of the same model sits poorly parked in the street. The vinyl roof has holes in it, and both bumpers have significant scarring. One of the doors on Jim's car is the color of primer, and only two wheels on the car match. On the broken windshield Jim scribbled the words, "If you can haul it, you can have it!"

Okay, so this story is one I made up, but I want you to see what a difference a little investment makes. The reason that Bob loves his car so much is that for ten years he has invested in it. He's taken care of issues when they've surfaced, he's done regular maintenance on his vehicle, and he's never been lax in the area of showing this vehicle tender-loving care. The reason that Jim eventually wants to get rid of his vehicle is that he never *really* invested in it.

In the Bible, God gives us a basic principle that explains the dynamic I was just illustrating:

> *Matthew 6:21 (NLT)*
> *21 Wherever your treasure is, there the desires of your heart will also be.*

In this passage, Jesus is talking about the fact that we should be investing our resources in things of eternal significance—not to gain earthly things that won't last. But I would like to take a moment and just focus on the axiom for life Jesus has just given. When Jesus tells us that our heart will be where our "treasure" is, I believe He is telling us that *our heart will always follow our investment.* If you want to know what you will eventually love more than anything, just figure out what you're investing in the most. If your resources in life — time, energy, love, focus, skill, money — were all stored up in one "checking account," to whom or to what are you writing the biggest checks? That is whom or what you will end up loving more than anything.

As a couple's coach, I've heard people talk about "falling in love" and "falling out of love" a lot. No wonder our relationships are struggling. If we talk about love like it's something we can "fall into" or "fall out of," we surrender control of the future of our marriages. If love is something we can "fall out of," then none of us has any business vowing on our wedding day to "love and to cherish" our spouse for the rest of our lives. *Love isn't about "falling," it's about investing.* The next time someone tells you that they fell out of love, you just give them the happy news that it's simpler than that... they fell out of investment.

No matter who you are, you have a lot of resources at your disposal. You have the ability to invest extravagantly in your spouse. You can give them your time, your energy, your listening ear, your shoulder to cry on, your words of comfort or reassurance — even simply your presence. All of these things constitute an investment that engages your heart. God even designed us to give our bodies to each other in the act of sexual intimacy. I believe that one of the reasons God has designed us to share ourselves with each other in this most intimate way is because it is, per-haps, the deepest way to engage one's heart. If you doubt this, you should ask a betrayed spouse how deeply their heart was wounded when their spouse shared themselves sexually with someone else.

Often I work with couples who complain of a "loss of feeling" in the relationship. They'll say, "We love each other, we're just not *in love* with each other anymore." Or, "We just don't have the feelings we used to have for each other." For these couples, these concerns are debilitating. After all, at one point they were passionate about each other. Now the passion has cooled, and they are left with a relationship that feels empty and unfulfilling. The good news for these couples is that the problem is as easy to fix as it was broken. What caused them to lose "feeling" in the relationship was their choice to stop investing.

Jesus is clear in Matthew 6: *Investment comes first; desire comes as a result.* Like many things in life, what makes the difference is the order of operations. We can either invest in the things we feel love for—which guarantees your feelings will be in control of your life, or you can invest in the things you want to feel love for—which puts your personal choice in the driver's seat. There's good news here: you can choose whom to love. If you feel like you're falling out of love with your spouse, be encouraged! You can choose to love your spouse—you *must* choose to love your spouse. Start investing!

Speak up! Your spouse won't know you want them unless you tell them.

As a young man, I had a tremendous "crush" on the woman who would later be my wife. Wendy is a bit older than me, though, and back then, I knew that I had no chance at winning her attention. She was interested in older guys... guys that shaved, and drove cars and so forth. My love for Wendy back then was *love from afar*. Years later, after attending college, Wendy and I bumped into each other after a church service. There was something special about that meeting, and it wasn't too long before we were spending time together.

Part of what changed the nature of our relationship and allowed us to grow close was the fact that we both *expressed* a desire to be with each other. It was our willingness to tell each other that we wanted to be together that made our new relationship different from what I had felt years ago. Now instead of love from afar, it was up-close-and-personal love. There's something about actually speaking the words, "I love you and I want to be with you," that gives a relationship a chance to grow closer.

I work with too many couples that have almost everything going for them, yet their love is *from afar*. They have stopped *expressing* their desire for each other, because they each think the other person *already knows*. I remember one gentlemen in particular who said to me, "She knows I love her! I've told her a bunch of times." But after I spent some time with this precious couple, it became clear that the *real* expressions of love ended some time ago. Now when he says, "I love you" to his wife it's at predictable times and with somewhat diminished feeling. He says "I love you" when he leaves the house or hangs up the phone, or after sex. His wife is used to hearing I love you at these moments, and is now wondering if he really desires to be with her.

Your spouse will *always* need to receive your expressions of love, no matter how many times you've communicated it before. These expressions of love will have no effect if they become part of some stale routine. They must be real and from the heart. Your spouse knows the difference between when you really mean something and when you just say something for effect.

One additional thought: Be creative! You know a lot about your spouse, and the longer you live with them, the more you'll learn. Each of us receives expressions of love in different ways. Do something more than just *saying* you love your spouse. Find out what really "rings their bell" in terms of receiving love. Maybe your spouse really lights up and receives your love when you do something romantic that shows them you're thinking of them — like leaving love notes or planning little surprises.

Maybe your spouse is overcome by feelings of your love for them when you are sexually intimate with them. Perhaps your spouse feels loved most when you spend time doing things together. Take some time and learn how your spouse receives love. Once you know how to "ring their bell" you can become a double threat — you can continue to speak your love for them and show it at the same time. That would be a game changer!

BE THE MASTER OF THE "WISH LIST"

No matter what you have going on in your life, you are the one who controls what you wish for. You are in the driver's seat. To a great extent, the decisions you make right now regarding your wish list will determine the course of your future. It's much too easy to let life control your list. It's tempting to let your feelings start calling the shots, but you *must* take control… you must take charge. It's your wish list.

Some time ago your spouse captured your heart. Does it still belong to them? Do you still desire them more than anything else in the world? If not, what is keeping them from having that special place in your heart and mind? What distractions or outside investments are causing you to let your heart wander? Don't let Satan tempt you to drift away from the God-given beauty of your relationship. Maybe today would be a great day to let your spouse know that you still desire them. They belong at the top of your wish list. Make a choice to do everything in your power to keep them there.

Dear God,
Distractions are all around me. They call to me and demand my time and attention. Please help me to remember how important it is to focus on my spouse — the love of my life. Show me ways to communicate my desire for them. I don't want to fall out of investment — help me put my "treasure" where I would like my heart to be. Teach me how to express my love for my spouse — You've certainly expressed Your love for me.

Chapter 9

MAPPING THE "MINEFIELD"

I hope as you've read the pages of this book that you've felt the "blindfolds" in your relationship falling away. Maybe as you re-discovered the importance of concepts like trust, support, or desire, you've identified some of the root causes of difficulties you and your spouse have experienced. Now, we turn a bit of a corner, because in this chapter, we're focusing on taking what we've learned in the last seven chapters and putting it to good use in your relationship. You may remember that in Chapter 1 we talked about *"navigating the minefield."* We said that it's often easy to be "blown up" by your spouse when you step on the wrong trigger.

Just as people don't go looking for landmines to step on, most of us truly do not go looking for fights. Like a hidden explosive waiting to be triggered, many fights in our marriage lie just beneath the surface ready to ignite at any moment. Where do they come from? And, perhaps more importantly, how do you deal with them? In this chapter, we'll discuss the sources of the landmines in your relationship, how you can identify the triggers, and how to harness the explosive power of potential conflict.

WHAT THE LANDMINES ARE (WHY SMALL ISSUES CAUSE BIG EXPLOSIONS)

In the last seven chapters we've discussed your spouse's seven major needs. You trigger a landmine in the relationship by saying or doing something that leaves your spouse missing one of these major elements. When your spouse feels they can't trust you, that you won't be there for them, that you won't comfort them when they experience pain, that you won't support them in their life's pursuits, that you don't accept them, that you won't respect them, or that you don't desire them, you can expect something to explode. It's my hope that having read the last seven chapters, you can now look back at any major fight that you have had with your spouse and identify which of those issues caused the conflict.

You may have noticed, though, that little things have the ability to very easily trigger these big landmines. Small conflicts about relatively inconsequential issues like whether or not to paint your living room, how much money you should spend on vacation this year, or who decides where you'll eat dinner tonight can trigger big landmines. This is a constant source of frustration for many couples. They voice questions like, "Why do we always fight about stupid little stuff that doesn't even matter?"

Here's the answer: they don't fight about little stuff. They fight about big stuff. They just don't realize what they're really fighting about.

So What Is The Fight About?

The fight is about a behavior, right? After all, isn't the fight about a wife's compulsive desire to paint every room in the house every year, or a husband's out-of-control spending, or the fact that neither of them have any desire to pick a restaurant to eat at tonight? Nope. Behaviors aren't near important enough to cause the kind of emotional upheaval we experience when we're in the throes of a nasty fight. It's what's *underneath* the behaviors—beliefs.

Right now as I'm writing this book, I have no desire to hop up out of my chair and stand on the other side of the room. However, if you were to convince me—to get me to believe—that a 3000-volt electric shock was about to be applied to my chair, you'd see me vacate my seat very quickly. My belief (that I was getting ready to be fried by an enormous amount of electricity) commanded my behavior (jumping out of the chair). It works the same way in marriage. Our beliefs inspire—and to some extent dictate—our behaviors. I believe this is why God invites us to a relationship based first and foremost on belief. The Bible is clear… when we believe in God, our behavior changes as a result. Behavior always follows belief.

When you see two people in an intense marital fight, you're not just seeing two people behaving badly, you're seeing two people overwhelmed by negative beliefs. Both individuals are completely overtaken by negative feelings that are causing them to be very desperate. Why is it so easy for us to become flooded with negative beliefs? The answer is found in something scientists refer to as "confirmation bias." Stay with me for a minute while I explain this concept, because it could forever change your view of the conflict in your marriage.

I like to refer to confirmation bias as the "I told me so" effect. Basically this scientific theory states that once we come to a certain belief (like "my spouse doesn't really care how I feel") we will pay attention to evidence that proves our belief correct, and ignore evidence that may prove us wrong. Think about how powerful this effect can be in marriage. Say you come to a *momentary* belief in a heated argument that your spouse doesn't respect you. The theory of confirmation bias suggests that in that moment you will be flooded by evidence that proves you are right. You will remember all the times your spouse was disrespectful, while ignoring the memories of times they did respect you. This is why I call this the "I told me so" effect.

So many couples who do have great trust relationships have huge fights about trust. Lots of couples who respect each other deeply have terrible conflicts where they accuse each other of having no respect. Why? Because when we come to that momentary belief—"I can't trust them" or "they won't support me," etc.—we get stuck in a feedback loop of convincing evidence that causes us to feel absolutely justified about our characterization of our spouse.

Life In The Echo Chamber

Scientists who study sound have constructed something called an "echo chamber." In this special spherical room, sounds bounce off the round walls creating repetitive and recursive echoes. Once a sound is made, you'll hear that sound over and over again. This is what happens to us in a fight when we come to a belief like "my spouse doesn't really love me." It is as though that thought creates the original sound in our own personal "echo chamber" and thereafter, those messages repeat so often and so loudly that we cannot hear the voice of reason.

For Example...

Roy and Samantha decide to eat dinner at a local restaurant, arriving just before the evening rush. When the waitress came out, Roy commented on her unique name. "Orchid—what an unusual but pretty name," he said. The waitress seemed to key off of his complement for the rest of the evening. Samantha had never had any reason to suspect her husband of being interested in another woman, but she was a bit uncomfortable with his remark about the waitress's name. "When has he ever said anything about how wonderful my name is?" she wondered. For the rest of the meal, the young attractive waitress seemed to pay an inordinate amount of attention to Roy while not paying attention to Samantha, or other guests. She asked Roy multiple times if his meal was alright, and asked to refill his drink half a dozen times. Meanwhile, Samantha's glass sat on the table empty.

Well, our waitress certainly seems taken with my husband, she thought. As she sat and contemplated the situation, she became angry. She tried to be civil with the waitress when she finally asked about refilling her drink, but it was a lost effort. She unloaded on the young woman about all of the mistakes she had made that evening. She didn't mention anything about the fact that the young woman was making eyes at her husband, but she definitely criticized the waitress for everything else she had done wrong. Meanwhile, Roy was becoming irate with Samantha. How dare she speak to a waitress with such hostility and contempt? After all, the woman was just doing her job.

When the check came to the table, Samantha remarked to Roy, "Well, we know one waitress who won't be receiving a good tip tonight."

That was about all Roy could take. He quickly designated a twenty-five percent tip on the receipt and signed it with an ostentatious flourish. *That will show her to try to control me,* he thought.

When Samantha saw the tip amount, she flipped out. She became even more angry and hostile, and began yelling at Roy. Before the evening was over, Roy and Samantha engaged in an all-out shouting match in the middle of their favorite restaurant.

Later, as they tried to process what had happened at the restaurant, they couldn't believe how such a small thing—a simple tip amount—could end up causing them to behave so irrationally. They were shouting at each other in a public place. In hindsight, it seemed like a crazy thing to do. When they came to see me for marriage coaching, they said, "It was such a small thing—why was it such a big fight? Why did things get so out of control?"

Simple. When Samantha heard her husband compliment the waitress, and then saw the waitress paying attention to her husband, she accepted momentarily the belief that her husband might be drawn to another woman. Because she accepted that belief, she was immediately flooded with any evidence her brain could produce and catalog that proved her right. She was stuck in the echo chamber. It was as though her mind was filled with the repetitive sound: *your husband will be interested in this woman... he's not interested in you... he wants to be with her... you're not good enough for him.* The "echoes" of these thoughts drown out all the evidence to the contrary. She cannot in that moment hear the voice of reason—that her husband has given her evidence to believe that he's only interested in her, and that she *is* "good enough" for him.

That's why she demanded the tip amount be low, even though she really couldn't care less how much her husband tips. If you were to find Samantha on a normal day—a day when she isn't trapped in the echo chamber—and ask her if she believed her husband would be faithful to her, she would answer with an unequivocal "yes." But in the moment—at the restaurant—Samantha is stuck in the echo chamber. All she can hear are the voices that tell her she should fear losing her husband. As a result, she acts out of character. She feels angry and hostile at the prospect of having her husband taken away from her.

Roy is also in the echo chamber. Inside his head, the message, "she's trying to control you" repeats non-stop. When Samantha indicates to him that the waitress "would not be getting a good tip," Roy feels as though Samantha is treating him like a child. As a result, his mind is flooded with examples of ways in which his wife has tried to control him or is currently controlling him. In that moment, trapped in the uncontrollable loop of negative dominating emotions, he's convinced that his wife is the enemy. Ask Roy on a normal day if his wife is a manipulative controlling person and he'll answer quickly "of course not." Samantha is respectful and supportive, but in this moment, Roy is flooded by feelings that she might not be. That's why he's so upset.

Anytime a fight in your relationship is about something "small," but has become a "huge" conflict, you're dealing with something bigger than the "issue" at hand. If you're having a knock-down-drag-out fight about whether or not to buy something, whether or not to take the kids to this or that event, or where to eat lunch, you should already be realizing that the fight is about something bigger. What's it about? Negative beliefs. Which negative beliefs? The ones we've been combatting in the last seven chapters.

Is your spouse desperately upset at you? Then they've more than likely come to believe one or more of the following:

- they can't trust you
- you won't be there for them
- they will have to endure pain or fear alone
- you won't support them as they take on life's challenges
- you can't accept them, you don't respect them
- that you don't desire to be with them

Realizing this may give you the ability to quit arguing about unimportant things and talk about what's really important. The couple who found themselves in a big fight about a tip at a restaurant need to realize that the very fact that it is a "big fight" means that they are fighting about something bigger than a tip.

Little landmine triggers can create big explosions. One act of deception can trigger your spouse's "trust" landmine and cause them to believe they can't trust you. One incident of not being there for your spouse in a moment of pain can leave them in a full-blown panic believing you will never be there for them. *If your spouse is triggered into a feedback loop of negative beliefs you* must not argue with them. We talked a bit about this in a previous chapter when we talked about not approaching an emotional battle armed with logic. The point of this book is to give you a glimpse into your spouse's world… to help you understand the pain and fear they experience when they are triggered into that tsunami of negative emotion.

You could argue with your spouse when they experience one of these terrible moments… you could try to explain to them how you are being unjustly accused and inaccurately labeled. Just realize that if the laws of confirmation bias hold true, it is very unlikely that they will be able to accept any argument you offer. You'll most likely just make them more desperate. It is incredibly important to be aware of what your spouse is going through in those moments. Identify the landmine(s) you have stepped on, then do your very best to understand the pain or fear. Arguing won't help; distancing will make it worse. Engaging is the one thing you can do that will give your spouse the safe base they need.

HOW THE LANDMINES GOT THERE
(YOU MAY BE SURPRISED TO KNOW THAT IT'S NOT ALL YOUR FAULT.)

The Pain of the Past

One of the most challenging aspects of my work with couples is helping them recognize that many of the "triggers" in their relationship were there before they ever met. If you're like Wendy and I, you and your spouse didn't start spending time together until after you had entered adulthood. Just think of all the life you had already experienced before meeting your spouse. The truth is that there were "landmines" in your life and in the life of your spouse before you ever started interacting with each other.

Imagine a little girl—six years old—who must often cope with being abandoned. Her mother left her father when she was four, and now her father's drug habit ensures that most of the time she is left alone with no one to care for her. Often, her dad gets mad at her for no reason and yells at her before marching out the door, slamming it behind him. When he walks out, she has no idea when he will return—or in what condition. Every time he leaves, she is left with an overwhelming sense of fear and pain. *Will he come back? Why would he leave me? What did I do wrong?* No little girl should have to feel this way. As the years go by, she becomes very strong and independent—she had no choice. Now when her father leaves, she doesn't cry and tremble in fear as she did years ago. As a teenager, she yells and screams in anger, berating her father for treating her this way.

Now, fast forward to this young lady's life as an adult. At thirty, she is married to a wonderful man who is nothing like her sad excuse for a father. This man loves her deeply and they are working very hard at making a wonderful life together. The problem is that sometimes they have pretty intense arguments. When they argue, he feels overwhelmed and tries to walk away from her (after all, he has his own past, and his own minefield to deal with). Because she continues to pursue him, he usually heads for the door. When this happens, she unleashes her anger in his direction in a way that would shock anyone.

This man loves her very much. He would do anything for her. He just hasn't mapped the minefield—he hasn't discovered the triggers in his marriage. He doesn't realize that every time he walks toward that door, he forces his wife back into that traumatic place she experienced as a little girl. He didn't create this trigger, but accidentally stepping on it *is* something he must learn not to do. If this man were reading this book, he may well feel that he meets her needs in all of the seven basic areas we've discussed. The problem is that earlier in her life, someone violated almost all of them. For him, mapping the mine-field in his relationship must start with a realization of how he is accidentally creating new situations that force her into old pain.

Fortunately, most of us do not have stories of past trauma as substantial as the one I just mentioned, but all of us do have past wounds that impact our present behavior. It is all too easy for a married couple to gloss over their his-tory and not fully explore each other's past. I do a form of marriage coaching I call "intensive coaching," where I spend an entire day with one couple. Part of the usual intensive routine centers on a brief discussion of how each individual grew up. We discuss the pains and difficul-ties as well as the victories and good moments of those days. We also spend some time discussing prior romantic relationships, which also are a frequent source of past pain. What is amazing to me is that almost every time in these appointments, couples that have been married for years discover something new about each other — some-thing crucial that impacts their marriage. In six hours, it seems we have unearthed something that hasn't been talked about for ten years or more. That doesn't seem right.

What do you not know about your spouse's history? Would you be able to accurately guess the most painful moment they lived through before they met you? Could you accurately guess their biggest fear as a child? If you don't know these things, you should. Understanding what the "minefield" looked like before you showed up is very helpful. This can actually be a huge source of encouragement for you both. It might just be that some of what you are going through right now as a couple stems from past pain that neither of you caused. By exploring some of these past issues, you have the opportunity to create a new emotional environment of safety, and make sense of what previously felt like a crazy part of your relationship.

Present Pain From Other Sources

Another way that landmines end up in our spouse's life is through pain or fear inspired by other sources. Maybe your spouse's occupation is doing a great job of putting landmines in their life, or maybe a family member or friend is creating unnecessary pain. Maybe your spouse is going through physical or emotional pain that stems from health issues. Regardless, there are many ways in which your spouse can be experiencing pain right now from sources other than you.

As we discussed in the last section, just because you didn't create the trigger doesn't mean that you won't step on it. This is why it is so vital for both parties in the marriage to understand the everyday pain and stress the other person encounters. If we are not listening when our spouse shares what they are going through we run the risk of ignoring huge triggers in their life.

One man — we'll call him Dave — was going through the pain of a shakeup at his office. It looked as though he might lose his job, or have his compensation cut. Either way, his ability to face the future with confidence was quickly disappearing. The ominous announcement came on a Tuesday.

"We're having a meeting tomorrow to discuss some restructuring," his boss said.

He knew what that meant. Life would be different for his entire family starting the next day. He and his wife had plans to eat with friends that night, and he didn't want to ruin the evening. Still he had to say something. He tried to gently mention the problem to his wife as she got the kids ready for the babysitter and finished curling her hair. Not really hearing what he was saying, she asked, "Can we talk about this later?" He nodded.

At dinner that evening, their friend talked about his new position at a software programming company. Throughout the evening, Dave's wife congratulated their friend again and again for having found a new successful career. She even made a remark about how long Dave had been "stuck" in the same department for years doing the same boring job. By the time Dave and his wife prepared to leave for the evening, Dave's blood pressure was high enough to get him admitted to an emergency room.

Here I am worrying about losing my job, and my wife can't stop criticizing it. She doesn't appreciate me or what I do, he thinks. In anger, he refused to speak to his wife for days. She didn't know why he was so mad. She asked several times but was met with icy silence. She meant no harm, but she stepped on a landmine that pushed Dave deeply into the pain of his current stressful situation.

As a husband, I am tremendously concerned that many times my wife tries to communicate the difficulties of her present situation and often I simply do not hear them. It's too easy to let my own concerns and workload drown out the sound of her voice as she tries diligently to share with me her problems and hurts. Just as Dave's wife didn't have any clue that her remarks would trigger debilitating pain for her husband, often I don't know enough about what Wendy is going through *right now* to understand why I sometimes cause her to be triggered into hurt or pain. To keep us from falling into this kind of insensitivity, the Scriptures remind us to "share each other's burdens."

Galatians 6:2 (NLT)
2 Share each other's burdens, and in this way obey the law of Christ.

We were not meant to live life alone. As we discussed in Chapter 3, we are to be a lifeline for each other. We can't do that if we don't know what the other person is living through. We cannot ignore our spouse's life struggles and challenges simply because we have our own problems.

Sharing each other's burdens gives us an awareness of the dangers we face as a couple. As we've already stressed elsewhere in the book, if your spouse has a problem, you have a problem. God has merged you into a new entity of one (Matt. 19:6), and, as a result, you are responsible to be concerned not only about your own problems, but about your spouse's as well.

Sinful Life Patterns (Some of it could be you.)

In the book of Psalms, David asks God to examine him carefully to see if there might be any "offensive" way in him.

Psalm 139:24 (HCSB)
24 See if there is any offensive way in me;
lead me in the everlasting way.

The word rendered "offensive" in this text is a Hebrew word that means "hurtful to another person." David is acknowledging that it is possible that some feature of his person might be hurtful to God or others. This humble acknowledgment is at the center of all healing in relationships. Now, we must be careful not to take responsibility for every pain and difficulty our significant other experiences. As we have said previously in this chapter, there are often other causes for the hardships we encounter. However, we must always be open to the realization that there may be something about the way we live our lives that is dishonoring to God and hurtful to others.

David is asking God to examine his heart carefully and reveal these areas. In his request is the distinct implication that if God were to reveal areas of his life that are deficient, he (David) would work diligently to grow out of those life patterns through God's power. This is a commitment that we must choose to make if we want to see our marriage relationships move forward. We must be committed to: first, to be open to understand the ways in which we may be hurting our spouse, and second, be unwavering in our efforts to grow personally in those areas where we are struggling.

Consider the man who has spent years of his life secretly addicted to pornography. His wife's deep and abiding pain that results from discovering this infidelity and deception is a direct result of her husband's sinful pattern. If their relationship has hope of moving forward, he must be willing to realize that this *is* a pattern of sin in his life, and he must be fully committed to a growth journey that targets not only his full recovery, but also his personal growth in the area of purity and faithfulness.

Or, on a lesser scale, consider a woman who has spent years of her life berating and verbally abusing the people she claims to "love." If the close relationships in her life ever have a chance of healing, it will start with her willingness to understand that she has fostered a pattern of sin in her life. Confronting that truth, and being willing to work diligently to learn new ways of communicating and expressing her feelings will put her on the fast track to seeing her relationships in a different light. Additionally, it will give the people in her close circle the chance to get to know and love her.

When you recognize that you have somehow "stepped on a landmine" in the relationship, and things are getting explosive between you and your spouse, be open to the possibility that this landmine represents an area where you have some growing to do. Perhaps the explosion you are experiencing is the result of a pattern of hurtful behavior in your life. Let's face it… we all have our personal struggles and difficulties. The fact that you have your own patterns to conquer doesn't make you a terrible person — it makes you human. It is what you do with these patterns that will determine your ultimate success or failure in life and relationships.

> *Romans 12:1–2 (NLT)*
> *And so, dear brothers and sisters, I plead with you to give your bodies to God because of all he has done for you. Let them be a living and holy sacrifice — the kind he will find acceptable. This is truly the way to worship him. 2 Don't copy the behavior and customs of this world, but let God transform you into a new person by changing the way you think. Then you will learn to know God's will for you, which is good and pleasing and perfect.*

WHEN MY SPOUSE IS IN THE "ECHO CHAMBER"... WHAT SHOULD I DO?

Go There With Them...

As we said earlier in this chapter, it is definitely counterproductive to *argue* with your spouse when they are in the echo chamber. Their mind is flooded with negative thoughts when this happens, and you trying to interject your positive or problem-solving point of view will not help. As a matter of fact, they will push back against your point of view which will likely make you mad, and in the end, you will both be very upset. The best thing you can do when your spouse is triggered into the flood of negative thoughts and is stuck in the "echo chamber" is to be willing to go there with them.

By "going there with them," I mean listening to what they have to say *whether or not you have good reasons to disagree with them.* It's fine for you to understand that you don't agree with their point of view (which — let's remember — is irrational at that moment anyway), but you will get much further at this moment by listening than by refuting. If you push back against how they are feeling (even if you have a good reason to push back) you will leave them feeling like they are alone and misunderstood. Instead, when you hear your spouse out, you are *going with them* into that dark, emotionally frightening place. You are showing them that you care about what they feel.

The second part of "going there with them" is empathizing. When you see the word "empathy" or "empathizing" in this book, I am referring to the ability to temporarily see the world as your spouse sees it. Pardon the cliché, but empathizing means putting yourself in your spouse's "shoes." Being willing to experience the current situation the way they experience it. It means being humble enough to temporarily set your own feelings aside and experience your spouse's feelings. I said that empathy is the second step and not the first, because you can't empathize unless you listen. Good listening skills will give you the information necessary to do the hard work of empathizing. Listen first, then do your best to feel what they are feeling.

By hearing your spouse out and empathizing with what they are going through, you enter the "echo chamber" with them. As a result, they will know that you are capable of seeing what they are going through, and while you may never fully understand their pain, you can relate because you have tried to feel what they feel. When you try this, don't be surprised if your spouse seems a little shocked at first. Since none of us do this "listening and empathizing" thing naturally, it may take some practice on your part, and it may take your spouse a little while to believe what you're doing is genuine. Don't give up. No one wants to experience the echo chamber alone. When you are willing to face the negative messages of life *with* your spouse, you become an ally, not a combatant.

It is then—when your spouse is able to understand that you understand them—that you will find a freedom you may have not felt in your marriage up until now. It is then that your spouse can begin to hear your thoughts, concerns, and opinions. By showing your spouse that you can identify with how they feel, you inspire them to believe that they are not alone and that you care. When your spouse feels that you truly understand them, it's as though they are able to exit the echo chamber with you and begin opening their mind and heart to outside messages. In those moments of mutual understanding, amazing things happen.

Dear God,
Please bring healing to our relationship. Help me to understand what my spouse is going through when they are flooded with negative thoughts and emotions. Help me to be there for them in those moments. I know that You can give us the strength to grow toward each other even through difficult circumstances. Thank You for taking us on that journey step by step.

Chapter 10

WHILE I'M WAITING

Recently, I walked the aisles of a local Christian bookstore. Since I was writing a Christian book on marriage, I decided to scan the shelves dedicated to books on marriage and relationships. As I thumbed through the pages of familiar books (many of which I had previously read in entirety), I noticed a common theme in many of them. "Do *XYZ*," the book would say, "and then your spouse will respond by becoming who you want them and need them to be." The message of many of these books seems to be, "If you do what this book tells you to do, your spouse is bound to come around." WRONG. It doesn't work that way.

Messages like these have intensely frustrated dozens of individuals I have eventually coached in my office. "I did everything the book said to do," they say, "and my spouse is still hurtful and vindictive." Or, they say, "I really tried my best to be the godly Christian spouse the book said I need to be, and my spouse is still addicted to pornography." I believe that the authors of these books mean well, but the message they are sharing sometimes does more damage than good. If you could get your spouse to do all the right things and become the person you want them to be simply by modifying your behavior, that would be manipulation. Your behavior change would be short lived even if you were able to get the result you wanted, and your spouse would eventually realize they were being played.

In Luke 15, Jesus tells a story about a son who had a rebellious spirit and chose to leave his home after demanding an early inheritance from his father. Once this young man was adequately situated with money, he ran far from home and squandered his father's wealth while creating a lifestyle that accentuated his rebellion. These actions likely wounded his father's heart. I'm a bit concerned that if the father in our story were to read a few self-help books now on the shelf, or receive advice from a well-meaning but misinformed Christian about his circumstance, he might hear the message: "just do _____ (fill in the blank), and your son will come around. He'll eventually respond to the fact that you're doing the right thing."

But notice when you read this story in the Bible that it was *not the father's behavior* that motivated the young man to come home. It was *his own realization* that he needed to repent—that he needed to walk away from the lifestyle that was causing pain not only to others, but also to himself.

> *Luke 15:17–19 (NLT)*
> *17 "When he finally came to his senses, he said to himself, 'At home even the hired servants have food enough to spare,*

and here I am dying of hunger! 18 I will go home to my father and say, "Father, I have sinned against both heaven and you, 19 and I am no longer worthy of being called your son. Please take me on as a hired servant." '

It was not a letter or communiqué from the father that changed this young man's heart. It was not that the father had learned new behaviors or techniques to "inspire" his son to want to return. It was the fact that the son "finally came to his senses." The son had experienced enough pain to be motivated to change his own lifestyle. If your spouse has traces of rebellion in their spirit, they will not be eradicated by some new behavior you learn or some new realization you adopt. Their behavior will change when they realize the pain they are causing themselves and others and when they are ready to make the changes necessary to move in the right direction. That's called repentance, and no one can do that for them. You can't repent for your spouse, and they can't repent for you. It's always a personal decision, and it always starts with the person that needs to repent.

SO WHAT CAN I DO TO MAKE A DIFFERENCE?

The prodigal son knew two things. The first was that he was experiencing personal pain as a result of his bad choices. The second was that "home" was a place he wanted to be.

Luke 15:17–19 (NLT)
17 "When he finally came to his senses, he said to himself,
'At home even the hired servants have food enough to
spare, *and here I am dying of hunger! 18* **I will go home…"'**
[emphasis added]

What was it that caused this rebellious kid to want to go home? Home was attractive to him because it was an environment where his needs would be met. He knew that even if he were to return as a servant, he would be fed and cared for. In short, his home was the *optimum environment* in which he could repent.

THE MARITAL "GREENHOUSE"

A greenhouse is a structure that provides an *optimum environment* for growth of plants that might not grow otherwise. I love raw tomatoes, especially ones that are allowed to ripen on the vine, but since tomatoes don't grow year-round, I am always a little depressed when the growing season is over. I remember though, as a child, visiting a friend's large industrial greenhouse. In the dead of winter, I walked past row upon row of bright red healthy tomato plants that were thriving inside the greenhouse. Away from the frigid weather and pesky animals and insects that might harm the plants, the tomatoes were growing beautifully.

Since then, I've always loved the idea of a greenhouse. I love the fact that the building provides an ideal environment for growth to happen. Here's the key, though: *the greenhouse doesn't guarantee growth.* You could have a batch of bad seed, or plants that just don't grow right. While the greenhouse does provide an optimum environment, the process still largely depends on the ability of the plants or seeds to produce. The best greenhouse in the world cannot take bad seed and turn it into good plants.

Hopefully, you're beginning to see the parallel here. This book strongly encourages you to invest your energy in becoming the spouse God wants you to be. In doing so, you create a *marital greenhouse*—an optimum environment for your spouse to grow and respond. But simply creating the greenhouse doesn't guarantee that your spouse will grow. Much still depends on their ability to recognize the areas in which they need to improve.

This is why you cannot take the "if-then" approach to resolving the issues in your marriage. You cannot take the stance of, "If I work out my anger issues with my spouse, then she will warm up to me sexually." Or, "If I work hard to respect my spouse, he will then respond by being there for me when I need him most." These "if-then" constructs will only leave you disappointed. The best way to look at your personal growth process in your marriage goes something like this: "I want to grow to become the kind of spouse God designed me to be, so that I can create the *optimum environment* for my spouse to grow with me *if they so choose.*"

The key is this: *Stop trying to grow the plant and start building the environment.* Many of us have squandered valuable days of our lives trying to *make our spouse grow.* We see an area in which we believe they are deficient or not meeting our needs, and we work hard to help them understand their personal failings and grow out of them. But remember, growth happens from the inside out, not from the outside in. You cannot make your spouse grow. All you can hope to do is create an environment that encourages growth. When as a child I saw that green-house, I knew that tomatoes were more likely to grow there than anywhere else in Wichita, Kansas. By developing an environment that meets your spouse's needs, you ensure that your spouse's personal growth is more likely to occur inside your relationship than anywhere else.

How Do I Build The Greenhouse?

Start with the core needs we've talked about in this book. Just creating an environment that is rich in trust, team-work, comfort, support, acceptance, respect, and intentional desire will go a long way to constructing your own mari-tal greenhouse. Like the prodigal son, your spouse may still choose to be rebellious. They may create distance or behave in ways that force you to create distance to protect yourself. In the end, though, you will have created the kind of environment that even a rebellious heart eventu-ally longs for.

Let It Be Their Choice

The father did not refuse the inheritance to his son, or block the doorway refusing to let him leave. Once the son took up residence in the far country, the father did not journey there to *rescue* his son from his own bad choices and bring him home. Rather, the father allowed his son to make his own choices. As a result, when the son made the choice to come home with a repentant heart, *it was his choice to do so.*

I hope you've read this book with *your own* personal growth primarily in mind, not the growth of your spouse, because this book is not a how-to manual with instructions to "fix" your husband or wife. No such guide could guarantee results, because *if your spouse truly "grows," it will have to be their choice.* None of us grow personally because our arm is twisted or because we feel compelled by another individual to grow in some way. We are willing to do the hard work of growing only after we recognize our need to do so.

SO... WHERE DO I GO FROM HERE?

Pray and Ask God to Speak to Your Spouse

If your spouse isn't open to hearing or receiving the truth today, that doesn't mean that their heart will always be closed to the truth. Give God a chance to work in their heart. Just be sure that you are ready to follow God's direction yourself. If you ask God to give your spouse an open heart, make sure you are working on having an open heart. If you ask God to help your spouse be less critical, examine your own patterns of communication. If you ask God to help your spouse to engage more and be an active part of the relationship, make sure that you are initiating engagement in your marriage.

> *Luke 6:39a, 41–42 (NLT)*
> *39 Then Jesus gave the following illustration: "Can one blind person lead another? Won't they both fall into a ditch?...*
> *41 "And why worry about a speck in your friend's eye when you have a log in your own? 42 How can you think of saying, 'Friend, let me help you get rid of that speck in your eye,' when you can't see past the log in your own eye? Hypocrite! First get rid of the log in your own eye; then you will see well enough to deal with the speck in your friend's eye.*

Get Help From a Godly Professional

Most of us are completely comfortable with calling in a "professional" when something is broken in our house that we don't know how to fix. Even if you're a "jack-of-all-trades," you know that there are some things you don't know how to fix, and that's when we pull out the yellow pages. We start looking for someone trained and experienced in dealing with the problem we are facing so that we can benefit from their expertise. How is your comfort level with calling a professional who can help you deal with the emotional problems you are facing? Are you open to getting help from an individual trained in stepping others through the process of personal growth?

If you and your spouse are experiencing struggles, and can't move past the place at which you are "stuck," why not consider working with a Christian marriage and family therapist, or professional counselor? If your spouse is unwilling to go, that shouldn't stop you. You can start going on your own. Perhaps your spouse's heart will warm up to the idea later. The key is to get the help *you* need now. Our country is full of Godly mental health professionals who can help you as you journey towards the personal growth you desire.

Embrace the Importance of Community

In your own personal growth journey, do not underestimate the power of healthy relationships. You and your spouse need to be surrounded by people who love and support you unconditionally. A great place to start looking for community is in your local church. Find out what your church offers in terms of small groups. Consider volunteering or serving in some capacity where you will make friends with other believers. Being able to be in a community of individuals who care about you and want the best for you will be a great asset as you seek to get closer to God and your spouse.

I do have one word of caution, though. *Be extremely careful that in your quest to build community that you do not open the door to an emotional or sexual affair.* Relationships developed in the process of building personal community should never border on romance. Friendships with members of the opposite sex should always be discontinued if your spouse feels uncomfortable with them.

Take Care of Yourself

God built you with three parts: body, soul and spirit. This means that in order to be "well," you must take care of yourself physically, emotionally, and spiritually. I want you to consider taking an inventory right now of where you are in all three of these areas.

Physically. Would your physician approve of the way you are treating your body right now? Are you eating right, getting the right amount of rest, paying attention to your body's illness or pain cues? Are you getting good exercise?

Emotionally. Imagine that your emotional life had a gauge like the fuel gauge on your dashboard in your car.

> "Full" indicates that you have a tremendous amount of emotional energy to take on life's challenges. You know what you are feeling throughout the course of the day, and you don't have problems expressing those feelings to others.

> "Empty" on the other hand indicates that you are completely emotionally exhausted. You have a hard time even knowing what you're truly feeling right now. It's even hard to tell others about your feelings because it's so difficult to put them into words.

Where would the "needle" on your "emotional gauge" point?

Spiritually. Where do you stand with God? Do you feel connected to God? Are you able to talk to God and sense His presence? Are you making time to read God's Word?

In the three areas we have mentioned — physical life, emotional life, and spiritual life — it is important to monitor your condition and pursue wellness. You may find that it's very easy right now to invest the majority of your time and effort in finding a way to connect with your spouse. It may be that your intense desire to be close to your spouse again inspired you to find the time to read this book. It's a good thing to be motivated to seek wellness in your relationships. Just don't allow your passion to "fix your relationship" to leave you numb to what you *must* do to remain whole and well as an individual. Allow God to work in your relationship as you seek His will. He can do amazing things!

Ephesians 3:20–21 (NLT)
20 Now all glory to God, who is able, through his mighty power at work within us, to accomplish infinitely more than we might ask or think. 21 Glory to him in the church and in Christ Jesus through all generations forever and ever! Amen.

A CONCLUDING NOTE
FROM THE AUTHOR:

God loves you and your spouse. No matter what difficulty you are going through right now, you can never lose God's love. While you take on the difficult task of evaluating your part in this relationship, ask God to superintend the process. Ask God to show you things that you are doing well, not just the things you are doing poorly. Ask God to help you celebrate the successes, not just grieve the losses. You are an incredible person. Even though I don't know you personally, I can tell you without reserve that you have much to offer. You have the potential to be an amazing spouse. God can help you become the person you hope to be. Lean on Him as you seek to find the path He has for you.

Proverbs 3:5–6 (HCSB)
5 Trust in the Lord with all your heart,
and do not rely on your own understanding;
6 think about Him in all your ways,
and He will guide you on the right paths.

I pray God's richest blessings on you and your marriage!

Jonathan Hoover

ACKNOWLEDGMENTS

Many people believed in me and supported this project, and it's impossible to list everyone. I was blessed by so many individuals, and for that, I am eternally thankful.

Wendy, thank you for being my true "helper" in life. Without your support and willingness to read my endless stream of rough drafts, this book would never have been possible. Thanks for refusing to let me quit or get down on myself. Thanks for believing that I had something to say. I love you with all my heart.

Tiffany Nix, you are an absolutely awesome editor. You caught the vision and helped me share this message in a clear and concise way. I am deeply indebted to you for your gracious and careful treatment of my manuscript.

TJ Nix, this book would never have the same impact without your fantastic cover design. God has truly given you an immense talent.

To the many people who have pushed me along the way to pursue God's true gifting in my life, and who have believed in me since day one, I cannot thank you enough. The list is long, but it includes *my two precious daughters, my parents, grandparents, and incredible in-laws.* The list also includes my *many therapist and psychologist friends,* who have shared insight and support along the way.

One name that especially belongs on this list is *Alan Day.* Alan was my pastor for six years, and the man who made the crazy decision to offer me a position on his church staff in 2007. Even though I didn't have the background or the pedigree, he saw potential in me. He sadly didn't live to know that I would eventually be working on this project, but I doubt this book ever would have been possible without his willingness to invest in me years ago.

NewSpring Church, I can't imagine pastoring a group of people who could love and support me any more than you do. You inspire me!

Almost everything I know about couples I learned from *couples.* At NewSpring, I've worked with so many couples over these past few years, and I want to thank each of them for their trust, openness, and flexibility. You have taught me much, and for that, I am extremely grateful.

Finally, but most importantly, I want to thank Jesus Christ, who is not only my Savior, but also the person who teaches me daily what real love is.

BIBLIOGRAPHY

Chapter Three

Ainsworth, Mary D. Infancy in Uganda; Infant Care and the Growth of Love. Baltimore,: Johns Hopkins Press, 1967.

Feeney, Brooke C. "The Dependency Paradox in Close Relationships: Accepting Dependence Promotes Independence." Journal of Personality and Social Psychology 92, no. 2 (2007): 268-285.

Gottman, John Mordechai. The Marriage Clinic : A Scientifically-Based Marital Therapy. New York: W. W. Norton, 1999.

Chapter Four

Coan, James A., Hillary S. Schaefer and Richard J. Davidson. "Lending a Hand: Social Regulation of the Neural Response to Threat." Psychological Science 17, no. 12 (2006): 1032-1039.

96313467R00134

Made in the USA
Columbia, SC
27 May 2018